War Year Champions

*The Welcome Diversion of the
1944 Green Bay Packers*

Tony Walter

M&B Global Solutions Inc.
Green Bay, Wisconsin (USA)

War Year Champions
The Welcome Diversion of the 1944 Green Bay Packers

© 2025 Tony Walter

First Edition

All Rights Reserved. The author grants no assignable permission to reproduce for resale or redistribution. This license is limited to the individual purchaser and does not extend to others. Permission to reproduce these materials for any other purpose must be obtained in writing from the publisher except for the use of brief quotations.

Disclaimer

The views expressed in this work are solely those of the author and do not necessarily reflect the views of the publisher, and the publisher hereby disclaims any responsibility for them. In the event you use any of the information in this book for yourself, which is your constitutional right, the author and the publisher assume no responsibility for your actions.

Front cover photo: Members of the 1944 Green Bay Packers celebrate in the locker room along with their coach, Curly Lambeau, after defeating the New York Giants in the NFL Championship Game. (*Photo courtesy of the Green Bay Packers*)

ISBN: 978-1-942731-54-2

Published by M&B Global Solutions Inc.
Green Bay, Wisconsin (USA)

Dedication

Authors often use their book dedication space to express thanks – perhaps to a teacher or mentor, to a family member – whose influence inspired the work. Then there are the times when research for the book produces a previously unseen admiration and appreciation for a society that served and endured through a period that later generations can't fully understand because they didn't live it with them.

This work pays due thanks to the men and women in the service in 1944, while also including those who had to navigate life at home and deal with issues supremely impacted by the war. These were people who carried with them the memories and effects of the Great Depression as they strived for a future that would offer promise and peace.

The 1944 Green Bay Packers season involved success on a football field. The coaches and players became idols to many for their accomplishments.

But the society of people, here and overseas, that lived through the same year became the heroes.

Contents

Prologue 1

January - *"The business of all the people"* 11

February - *"Spend, Sucker, Spend"* 27

March - *Victory Farms* 39

April - *Expand?* 49

May - *An Essential Difference* 59

June - *Throbbing Spectacle* 73

July - *Pollution at Bay Beach* 89

August - *Tail Gunner Joe* 101

September - *Football* 113

October - *Too Much Hutson* 127

November - *Little Boys Always Come Home to Cry* 145

December - *A Reverent Hush* 165

Player Biographies 189

Acknowledgements 205

About the Author 207

Prologue

The significance of that one day – December 7, 1943 – had to be apparent to anyone in the Green Bay, Wisconsin, vicinity, or anywhere in the world, for that matter. It was exactly two years since the Japanese attack on Pearl Harbor that changed so many lives and was still changing them.

"Where were you when you heard about it?" was a common question as individuals and families traced the changes in their own worlds over the previous twenty-four months.

But, as this Tuesday dawned, there were growing signs that the not-too-distant future – maybe even 1944 – might bring the world to the brink of this war's final chapter, at least against Germany, where the tide was ebbing further toward an Allied victory.

In fact, just the previous week, the executive committee of the Green Bay Chamber of Commerce met to form postwar planning committees. They identified six areas they wanted to address: employment, public works, private construction, wholesale and retail, agriculture, and public relations.

The residents of this northeastern Wisconsin community were keeping up with world developments through newspaper and radio reports. They were fed daily news about their sons and daughters in the military – who was killed, who was wounded, who was missing,

Franklin Roosevelt   **Joseph Stalin**   **Winston Churchill**

who was in a prisoner of war camp, who was promoted, who was a volunteer, who was home on furlough. It served as a valuable wartime scrapbook.

There was front page war news always. Readers of the *Green Bay Press-Gazette* learned that the three major decision makers (Franklin D. Roosevelt, Joseph Stalin and Winston Churchill) had just concluded their meeting at Teheran and let the world know that none of them would seek a separate peace treaty with Hitler and the Nazis, and that 1943 was certainly the final year of preparation for the invasion in Western Europe.

In the Pacific, the bombing of the Marshall Islands by US forces seemed to indicate that the next island-hopping step against the Japanese was close at hand, but most military minds were hesitant to predict a timetable for peace in Asia.

The War Manpower Commission said there would be no reductions in the military draft until at least February 1944, and the *USS Wisconsin*, one of the world's largest battleships, slid down the ways at the Philadelphia Navy Yard.

In Green Bay, the war's reverberations were everywhere, of course. On this day, Army Pvt. Milton Feldhausen's wife confirmed from her home on Cherry Street that she had been notified by the American Red Cross that he was a German prisoner of war after being captured in North Africa.

Cohen's Department Store, in business since 1887 and located at the intersection of Main and Jefferson streets, took out a full page ad in the *Press-Gazette* to urge customers to give war bonds as Christmas gifts rather than the store's merchandise.

The usual holiday-season gatherings were being planned, but with military overtones. The Battery Mothers would meet at the Legion building while the Jean Nicolet Chapter of the Daughters of the American Revolution would gather at the home of Mrs. O.C. Straubel.

Members of twenty-five bowling leagues in Green Bay proudly contributed $628 for the Bowlers Victory Legion fund to purchase recreation equipment for overseas servicemen. Sixteen women were being inducted into the US Marine Corps at the Hotel Northland and would help form an all-female platoon in the central states.

The film *The Battle of Russia* was showing at the Orpheum Theater. Moviegoers who wanted a different type of entertainment could go to the West Theatre and see Barbara Stanwyck and Henry Fonda in *You Belong to Me* or to the Bay Theater to see Humphrey Bogart in *Sahara*.

Fuel rationing during the war encouraged more traditional methods of transportation as evidenced by this horse-drawn delivery wagon used by the Rahr Brewing Company of Green Bay on November 1, 1943. (Green Bay Press-Gazette photo)

Workers remove the old streetcar rails from the Walnut Street Bridge in Green Bay on December 9, 1943. This two-lane bridge, built in 1910, remained in use until it was replaced in 1986. (Green Bay Press-Gazette photo)

Not everything was military-related in the Green Bay area that day. The city engineers said the old streetcar rails on the Walnut Street Bridge were finally scheduled to be cut away. The owners of two rural taverns were pleading not guilty to charges that they continued to serve alcohol after the 1 a.m. curfew. The Milwaukee Road announced that its popular Chippewa train would now leave the Green Bay depot nine minutes earlier than in the past. And the all-boys Central Catholic high school was getting ready to present the play *College Daze*.

A dozen waitresses at the Hotel Northland were guests for dinner at the hotel in recognition of their graduation from a vocational school course that taught them table serving methods, assisting in ordering, and sanitation.

The year was producing some impressive statistics: felonies and misdemeanors were only 62 percent of the number in Green Bay in 1942, and there was only one traffic fatality in the city in 1943 compared to nine the year before.

Green Bay and northeastern Wisconsin hadn't shirked their duties in providing manpower and financial resources for the country. They weren't spared the consequences of battle, either. There were sixteen Green Bay servicemen among the confirmed killed in 1943, with many more wounded or known to be prisoners of war.

The greater Green Bay community took home a commendable report card on home front support in 1943. It started a Victory Book drive in January, and registered 100 volunteers for Victory Garden space in April. Local druggists donated $350 of quinine for military use, and milkmen collected waste fat for the same purpose. Volunteers helped save the area cabbage crop, and even more stepped forward to help fill the empty work spaces in the area canneries. The region's first carload of valuable scrap tin cans was shipped out in February.

The area's third War Loan drive in the spring exceeded its goal, although the fourth drive in the fall came up $20,000 short of its quota.

The Green Bay district of the Smaller War Plant Corporation brought in $13 million of contracts and was able to complete the work faster than larger industries in many cases. The Ariens Company in nearby Brillion provided a good example when it produced the heavier armament for parachute troops.

The Chicago & North Western's new Streamliner visited Green Bay on January 9, 1942. (Green Bay Press-Gazette photo)

As the 1943 holiday season made its way into the battle-weary lives of everyone, the editorial writer for the *Press-Gazette* penned a message blended with hope and reality.

"The duty to make Christmas as real and bright as possible is a debt to both the present and the future," it read. "The tenets of Christianity are like unto the rugged cruisers that have carried us far over great waters and safely through black storms. Without them we are lost. With them it is possible for us to eventually march to triumph."

Green Bay was coping and Green Bay was hoping as history carried its citizens through daily unchartered territory that tested as it taught. Of course, every American community breathed the same wartime air.

But this was Green Bay and its DNA, wartime or not, set it apart

Don Hutson (left) signs a contract on December 11, 1943, to serve as an assistant coach to Curly Lambeau (right) for the 1944 season. Hutson ultimately decided to delay full-time coaching and went on to play two more seasons for the Packers while serving as an assistant coach. (Green Bay Press-Gazette photo)

Chicago Bears halfback Harry Clarke runs away from Green Bay Packers defender Charley Brock during the Bears' 21-7 victory at City Stadium in Green Bay. The game took place in front of a record crowd of 23,675 on September 27, 1943. (Green Bay Press-Gazette photo)

from everywhere else because it lived with a diversion unlike any other: the professional football delivered by the Green Bay Packers.

The 1943 Packers season, which ended just two days earlier, was unusual in several ways, impacted greatly by the war. The Packers finished 7-2-1, but played just two games in Green Bay.

The two losses were one-sided – falling 33-7 to the Washington Redskins and quarterback Sammie Baugh, and 21-7 to the Chicago Bears and quarterback Sid Luckman. None of the Packers' seven victories were close games.

The Packers set two attendance records, one for City Stadium in Green Bay (23,675 for the Bears game) and another at State Fair Park in Milwaukee (23,058 for the Redskins game).

Don Hutson, who said he played for the Packers in 1943 only because of the war-caused player shortage, would sign on a few days later as an assistant coach for the 1944 Packers. The implication was that he wouldn't play, but that remained to be seen. Every pro team was adjusting to the shortage of available players because of military enlistments. The Packers' final game was a victory over a Pennsylvania team that was a merged squad composed of Philadelphia Eagles and Pittsburgh Steelers.

The coming year would include increased pressure on the pro teams to find available players at a time when military manpower was the higher priority, and when more debate surfaced about the wisdom of even continuing pro sports at all during wartime.

Twelve of the Green Bay Packers' thirteen championship seasons have their identities attached to players or coaches. The first three titles (1929-31) were marked by the presence of Verne Lewellen, Johnny Blood, Mike Michalske and Cal Hubbard. Headlining the 1936 and 1939 title seasons were the accomplishments of Hutson, Clarke Hinkle and Arnie Herber. The 1960s and the five titles of that decade are known as the Lombardi dynasty. Brett Favre and Reggie White defined the team that won in 1996, and the 2010 championship has Aaron Rodgers' signature all over it.

What would be the identity and legacy of the 1944 Green Bay Packers as they took their place in pro football's wartime history? Who were the people who played pro football when there was a war that sapped manpower from everything non-military?

To fully grasp the identity of that 1944 team requires an understanding of the community that lived at its elbow.

It was a time of war fatigue mixed with post-war hopes, when a community's news and mood was delivered by a daily newspaper that tripled as a judge, a cheerleader, and a conscience to help its fellow citizens cope. Andrew (A.B.) Turnbull, as the newspaper's co-founder and publisher, had also served as president of the Packers, so his influence was evident in coverage of the team. Victor (V.I.) Minahan, co-founder and editor, directed the newsroom as it kept the community abreast of the war and its impact, and fed the readers the regular details of a football team aiming for another championship.

One person who had the *Press-Gazette* mailed to him every day was Maj. John Walter, my father, who was the orientation and com-

War Year Champions

Andrew Turnbull   **Victor Minahan**   **John Walter**
Green Bay Packers photo

munications officer at the US Army's Camp Wolters in Mineral Wells, Texas, about an hour west of Dallas. His interest in the Packers was natural, since he grew up in Green Bay and was the newspaper's sports editor from 1935 until being activated from the Army Reserves in October 1941. He was restricted to stateside military service because of health limitations that would eventually shorten his life.

One of Dad's daily duties in Texas was to produce a written update on the war for distribution throughout the base. To do this, he had access to the government's details of the war's progress. He would remain in Texas until being discharged as a lieutenant colonel in December 1945.

Dad's walk through the war details of 1944 coincided with the greater Green Bay community's walk through the same time period, with the names and places dedicated to memory for those who lived through it and parts of history for the rest of us.

These were the days before television and years before the internet fed the public information and tried to direct thoughts and votes. In Green Bay, the *Press-Gazette* provided the pictures, the context, and the details to keep the public up to date with the world, the country, and the community. Although the war steered the public compass, football salved the lifestyle as a welcome distraction.

This is the story of Green Bay and its Packers in 1944.

January 1944

"The business of all the people"

The brothers Smith took their wartime rationing reality to the advertising space of daily newspapers, including the *Green Bay Press-Gazette*.

Still selling, of course. But the public had to understand that even sore throats and nagging coughs weren't as important as the greater needs of a country in wartime.

"Please don't buy any more Smith Bros. Cough Drops than you need," it read. "Our output is wartime reduced and we're trying to offer everybody soothing relief from coughs due to colds. If you can't get Smith Bros. cough drops every time, get mad at Hitler. Smith Bros. have soothed coughs due to colds during five wars."

The ads did point out that both the black and menthol cough drop boxes were still a nickel each. (*Cough, cough*)

The cough drop advertisement was a fitting metaphor for the way a populace, in this case a business, was making prudent and unavoidable sacrifices in wartime while still trying to appear to be meeting the needs of public health and comfort, and its own bottom line. It was a tender balance.

Coping with the world war was primary, of course, but planning for the postwar period was already evident by this time and providing some hopeful glimpses to the future.

Just a week into the year, more than 100 Green Bay-area employers gathered at the Hotel Northland for dinner and to view *The War Department Reports* film about the war's progress. It was tickling with optimism after more than two years of finding traction against the enemies. The theme of the evening, highlighted by speaker Walter Schleiter of Chicago, was how Green Bay would fit into state and national postwar business models.

"Bold, intelligent, constructive plans must be made immediately by management to combat unemployment," Schleiter said. "If management doesn't solve the problems ahead now, the United States will either face mass unemployment or mass government employment after the war."

The Leathem Smith Shipbuilding Company in Sturgeon Bay, forty miles north of Green Bay, said it would offer $750 in war bonds to any employee submitting the most practical suggestions for postwar use of equipment and labor used in the present wartime shipbuilding program.

The current war and its progress was still the top story and dominated news, conversations and decisions. The daily reader's diet of printed articles about assignments and promotions of area servicemen and service women regularly mixed with somber notifications that the war's growing list of wounded, captured or killed included some Green Bay-area favorite sons.

There would be some distractions – statewide and locally.

As 1944 moved into its first month, steps were being taken that would have a huge impact on northeastern Wisconsin and its residents once the war was over. Most significant was the commitment of the state to relocate and reconstruct Highway 41 from Milwaukee to Green Bay, bypassing the downtowns of the cities between them. Once completed, it would reduce travel time for a populace that was destined to be more mobile once the limited purchase of gasoline and tires was no longer in force. Surveying was proceeding, but the construction would have to wait until materials and manpower were available after the war.

Local News Highlights

January 1: The first baby born in Green Bay in 1944 was Dorothy Ellen Jackson, daughter of Mr. and Mrs. Woodrow Jackson who lived at Twelfth Avenue. The baby's father was on duty with the navy and was aboard ship.

January 5: Peter Duquaine, Route 6, surprised each of his 10 children with a war bond as a Christmas gift.

January 10: A Nazi flag captured in the battle for Sicily was put on display at Franklin Junior High School by student Glen O'Dell, whose brother is in the service and sent it to him.

January 10: Three basketball players at Mountain High School, about an hour north of Green Bay, enlisted in the U.S. Navy over the holidays so the school's coach cancelled team's games for the rest of the season.

January 17: Hundreds of lost ration books dropped in the mail are being thrown away every month because the owners failed to fill in their address on the covers.

January 18: A new dairy transportation plan goes into effect for all Brown County dairy producers, processors and haulers, according to the Office of Defense Transportation. It aims to save 428,875 driving miles a year.

January 20: Visitors to the Bay Beach wildlife lagoons are asked to buy packages of corn from the vending machines there to feed the 272 ducks, 15 geese and three swans there. The park department budget doesn't include funds for feed.

January 29: Hundreds of Brown County residents who bought tickets to aid the victims of infantile paralysis danced at four locations to climax the week-long campaign.

January 31: Junior and senior high school girls from the Green Bay area will attend the first meeting of the YWCA's child class. A kindergarten teacher will speak on "Care of Infants and How to Entertain Small Children."

War had nothing to do with a liquidation sale of property in downtown Green Bay that drew some attention because it involved a landmark of sorts. The site of Bosse's News Depot on Cherry Street was purchased at auction for $37,175 by Mrs. Joseph Bosse, widow of the founder, because she wanted to protect the interests of the current operator, Norman Liebert, who had worked at the store for the past twenty-two years.

But war's shadow was everywhere, locally and worldly. The news fed the populace the financial impact – President Roosevelt wanted $100 billion more in the next eighteen months to keep the US military supplied – and there was human interest when someone interviewed young Lt. John Kennedy about his dramatic swim to safety after his PT boat was sunk.

And while the Selective Service guidelines were being expanded to include more fathers, enlistments in Green Bay for the new Women's Army Corps (WAC) platoon were also going up.

***

War didn't silence voices. Prodding, patience and pouting by the editorial writers at the *Press-Gazette* were in full force.

The Year That Lies Ahead
January 3, 1944

General Eisenhower prophesied that the war in Europe will come to an end in 1944. He put his prophecy among the possibilities by conditioning it upon the assumption that "every man and woman" in America can be induced "to do his or her full duty."

A year ago Admiral Halsey saw the end of the war in 1943. Perhaps we have not had a more capable sea dog since John Paul Jones than Halsey. But as a prophet he might have done better dancing the Highland Fling to the wild skirl of the bagpipes.

The Japs Change Our Gender
January 15, 1944

In recent years the Japs have classed the Germans and the Russians as masculine while we were rated as a feminine nation.

So profoundly did the Nipponese believe that their decision was correct that they are probably the most surprised people on the face of the earth today at the consequences every time our boys have clashed with theirs. For things feminine Japan has only contempt.

The Ones That Never Grew Up
January 5, 1944

As war was declared there was a very active and determined effort to close off all avenues of criticism as unpatriotic and partaking of an alliance with the devil.

It was thought that by stigmatizing as Hitler lovers those who saw and pointed to plain error the most glaring blunders of the inept and incompetent might be concealed from the public and eventually covered over with the dusts of time and thus forgotten.

Reformatory Schooling
January 8, 1944

The quality of inmates contained in the reformatory makes it evident that vocational training should be the basis and objective of the institution's operation. Yet, for the lack of a few thousand dollars ... the reformatory in 1944 has not yet begun to do the very job it was established to do nearly 50 years ago.

The Way of Defeat
January 10, 1944

The bombardment of our home front war complacency is getting heavy at Washington. But it is late and poorly aimed. The men at the front have no misconceptions about victory. They realize however far away it is.

Our home front is fairly rotten. And this in spite of the fact that a high percentage of the people are earnest, sincere and indefatigable in their efforts and purposes to support the army and navy.

This is No Time to Weary
January 19, 1944

We did not want this war. We did everything we could to awaken the people to the way we were drifting even as the President began to make commitments by sending his special ambassadors to Yugoslavia so long ago.

But the majority of the people did not believe with us. They elected to follow Mr. Roosevelt's promises never expecting they would find themselves in far places among alien peoples, there to leave their dead and eventually, in the fullness of time and victory, stray home, perhaps a wiser, certainly a sadder people.

***

The *Press-Gazette* had long ago been on record in opposition to the New Deal agenda and blamed Roosevelt's pre-war decisions as a contributing factor for getting the country into the conflict. But once the battles began, favorite sons became involved and the war progressed, the major theme promoted in the *Press-Gazette* was patriotism.

A January rally focused on the fourth War Bond campaign. Brown County was poised to meet its goal of $4,905,900, of which $3,833,865 was expected to come from Green Bay residents and businesses. Nearly 1,000 volunteers were set to begin the canvass of homes and industrial sites, with the deadline set for February 15.

More than 400 people – the majority of them women – were issued identification badges at a meeting at the Hotel Northland, designating them to canvass the neighborhoods as part of the Block Plan, a division of the Brown County Council of Defense. The canvass would also raise funds for the War Bond campaign.

The county's war finance committee trumpeted the call to action.

"We have just entered the crucial year of the war, a year of destiny, a year that promises to decide how good or bad a world we'll have to live in all the rest of our lives," read the statement. "This is as it should be. In a democracy, war is the business of all the people. Some must fight, some must work and put up the money."

There was good news when the national War Chest organization included Brown County as one of 404 communities in the country to exceed its quota when it raised six percent more than its $118,600 quota in the last three months of 1943.

There often were disagreements in the war coping process, though. The Office of Price Administration in Green Bay passed a rule permitting citizens to use some of their ration card points to purchase meat directly from area farmers. This bypassed the government inspection process, taking pressure off the area meat-packing plants that were struggling to keep up with the backlog of hogs and cows waiting to be butchered.

But Dr. George Shinners, the Green Bay Health Commissioner, said the new policy could result in people buying contaminated meat.

Occasionally, justice stepped in, if not very viciously. A farmer in Pound in Marinette County was fined just $1 and $12.95 in court costs for selling home-killed pork from house to house without collecting the required ration stamps.

Area farmers gathered at the Legion building for a two-day Brown County Victory Farm Institute where films such as *Soldiers of the Soil* and *Making Grass Silage* provided examples of farmers' contributions and solutions to war production. They were told of plans to use military-deferred single and married men on farms to cut pulpwood and lumber in the winter months so logging operations didn't lag.

Meanwhile, the Brown County Farm and Food Mobilization committee was formulating plans for a county-wide mobilization of citizens to meet the labor needs of food production for the coming season. The 1943 food production season was successful because enough people used their spare time to work in the fields or processing plants.

But the county's Office of Civilian Defense wasn't letting the public rest on its laurels. Marjorie Bidwell, chairman of the county's nutrition committee, declared a war on the waste of food. She said the "Clean Your Plate" drive would help reduce the amount of wasted food that was estimated at 300 pounds per person in 1943, food that was needed for the military.

Ed Holschuh, the town of Allouez garbage collector, said he still picked up about eleven barrels of wasted food a week from the 100 homes he served. Two-thirds of the waste was non-edible, but wasted bread and potatoes made up most of the rest of the tossed food.

The collection of scrap paper was organized for the first Saturday of the month, with 150 area Boy Scouts being driven in city trucks to pick up what residents put at the curb. The paper would become paperboard needed for containers in which such items as explosives and blood plasma are shipped to the armed forces.

The war also allowed some marital matters to be tweaked. Circuit Judge Henry Graass told the Fourteenth Judicial Circuit Bar Association at its meeting at the Beaumont Hotel that the Soldier and Sailors Relief Act made it possible for military men to get divorced without having to be present for the court proceedings. But a judgment couldn't be entered against them in their absence unless they waived the right.

A controversy arose after New Year's Eve when a local hotel proprietor was taken to court and charged with violating a city ordinance, modeled after a state law, that prohibited staying open after 1 am on New Year's Eve. Beaumont Hotel's A.C. Witteborg said it was unconstitutional because the state didn't hold Milwaukee County businesses to the same standard.

Hopes were high that the employment trend in 1943, which showed a 20 percent increase over 1942, would continue. But it was also assumed that building permits would continue to decrease because of the shortage of manpower.

***

As the year began, there was growing awareness that domination in the NFL was centered in Chicago, where the Bears had won cham-

Curly Lambeau stalks the sideline during the Packers' 25-17 loss to the visiting Chicago Bears at Green Bay's City Stadium on September 28, 1941. (Green Bay Press-Gazette photo)

pionships in three of the previous four seasons. They were expected to continue to challenge behind the league's most valuable player, quarterback Sid Luckman. The only uncertainty was Luckman's availability, as he enlisted in the Merchant Marines after the 1943 season.

The Packers had five titles in their pocket, but the last one was 1939 and the team that was expected to play in 1944 would have just eight players from that championship club: Charley Brock, Larry Craig, Buckets Goldenberg, Don Hutson, Harry Jacunski, Joe Laws, Baby Ray and Pete Tinsley.

The four seasons that followed the 1939 championship were winning regular seasons, but included little success against the Bears. The 1940 team went 6-4-1 and lost twice to the Bears. The 1941 team went 10-1 in the regular season (yes, that loss was to the Bears), then was drubbed by Chicago 33-14 in a playoff the week before the Bears hammered the Redskins 73-0 for the title.

The only two losses in 1942 were to the Bears, while the 1943 campaign at least provided improvement as the Packers tied one game against their rival and lost the other one.

However, since 1939, everything was second place.

January 1944 offered no Packers football games, but there was no shortage of stories related to the team – some unusual – and football people.

Lt. Cmdr. Jim Crowley, the former Green Bay East athlete, member of the Four Horsemen backfield at Notre Dame in the 1920s, and later head football coach at Fordham University, where he coached a lineman named Vince Lombardi, joined Admiral William Halsey's staff as welfare and recreation director for the entire Pacific theater.

Charley Brock, the Packers' outstanding center, decided to move to Green Bay because he couldn't find adequate housing in his hometown of Clarkson, Nebraska. He would spend the rest of his life in Green Bay.

There was a mini-controversy that involved fullback Ted Fritsch, who played for the Packers in 1942 and 1943. George Strickler, communications director for the National Football League, floated a rumor that Fritsch was the target of the University of Wisconsin, which wanted him to play for the Badgers. Fritsch was a student at UW-Madison, where he was getting a master's degree in physical education while working for a local dairy. The NFL investigated the rumor and found no evidence of a UW scheme.

In fact, a day or two later, Fritsch signed a baseball contract to play for the Los Angeles Angels of the Pacific Coast League, part of the Chicago Cubs farm system.

Ted Fritsch
(Press-Gazette photo)

Fritsch still intended to resume his career with the Packers in 1944, though.

Then there was the story about Babe Webb, a halfback who actually signed to play for the Packers in 1942 and 1943, but never showed up because he couldn't get transportation from Hawaii. Now living in Texas, Webb informed Lambeau that he would show up this time.

Lambeau knew he would be fielding players who might not be healthy enough to serve in the military.

"Strange as it may seem to most people," Lambeau said, "many boys who are physically capable of playing football cannot take the tough and grueling grind of maneuvers and actual battle. In most cases a lad has some minor injury which shows up when he joins service or when he is examined. He is released from service or rejected and yet he appears to be a fine physical specimen."

What lingered in the Packers offseason was the status of Hutson, the team's nine-year veteran receiver whose impact in the pro game was epochal. He appeared to be leaning toward retirement when the 1943 season ended and was immediately added to the team's coaching staff. But he had teased the public with retirement talk previously.

Hutson wasn't drafted after Pearl Harbor because he was married and had a child, so he wasn't classified 1-A. When the draft eligibility levels changed, Hutson was into his thirties and his status didn't change.

As a player, his reputation among opposing coaches and players put him in the elite class.

Pete Cawthon, coach of the Brooklyn Dodgers football team, had high praise for him.

"That fellow is uncanny," Cawthon said in mid-January. "I thought I had seen some good pass receivers until I saw Hutson. Now I know there is only one pass receiver and that's Hutson ... he's all by himself. His hands are so big and strong and skilled that Hutson can, and often does, catch a pass with one hand while warding off a would-be coverer with the other. I saw him do that against such a fine player as Pug Manders – and then apologize to Manders. It burned Pug up,

Curly Lambeau (from left) poses with Tony Canadeo, Andy Uram, Irv Comp and Don Hutson in 1943. Lambeau, Canadeo and Hutson are members of the Pro Football Hall of Fame. (Green Bay Press-Gazette photo)

but Hutson made the touchdown. It's only the young and the cocky who'll try (to cover him). The old heads just give up and frankly say they can't cover Hutson."

National columnist Grantland Rice wrote about whom he considered the greatest twelve football players who ever walked on a field.

"There could be no argument about such men as Jim Thorpe who could do everything," Rice wrote. "Bronko Nagurski, a great tackle, a great end and a great fullback. The same goes for Don Hutson, one of the most amazing of the entire crop."

Frankie Sinkwich, the former Georgia back who just finished his first season with the Detroit Lions, was also impressed.

"They (Packers) had more power and they had that Hutson, who is just absolutely the most amazing man I ever saw at catching passes."

The major pro football news as 1944 began involved the question of expansion. But the war ...

It had an impact on the NFL in 1943, with the Cleveland Rams sitting out the season and loaning several of its players to other pro teams. And the Pittsburgh Steelers and Philadelphia Eagles pooled their manpower into one team.

But attendance overall increased in 1943 so league owners, meeting in Chicago in the first month of 1944, revived discussion about expansion and hoped to return to a ten-team league in 1944.

Commissioner Elmer Layden said the growth of the league to new franchises was both inevitable and premature, although he hinted that expansion west was the likely direction.

The Boston Yanks had been awarded a franchise in 1943 but didn't field a team, although that was likely to change in 1944. Movie actor Don Ameche withdrew his application for a franchise in Buffalo, saying he hoped to get a team in Los Angeles instead.

After the war, league owners told him. After the war.

Layden said a decline in pro football popularity was predicted by some, but did not materialize.

"Here and there throughout the year certain observers, bemoaning the loss of stars, professed to see a decline ... but attendance figures seem to belie any inferiority in the caliber of league competition," he said. "Much of the increased enthusiasm ... stemmed from the balance in the league. In the main, the perennial leaders remained the leaders but their margins of superiority were reduced to a minimum. Further shrinkage in these margins can be expected next fall."

***

There were ways to escape war news temporarily. Entertainment for many came at the movie houses in Green Bay, where a variety was always available. On one January Saturday night, one could see John Wayne in *In Old Oklahoma* at the Bay, or James Stewart in *Mr. Smith Goes to Washington* at the West, or Jack Haley and Frank Sinatra in *Higher and Higher* at the Orpheum. Others chose to be entertained by Ethel Pagel at the piano at Smitty's Zuider Zee on Cedar Creek Road, later renamed Willow Street, and still later the current University Avenue.

The King of Clubs held its grand opening on Duck Creek Road

while Romy Gosz provided the music at Danceland Riverside on Main Street (later renamed Riverside Ballroom).

After the war, the debate between the margarine and butter proponents promised to eventually get resolved. A New York man took exception to the dairy forces in Wisconsin who claimed that margarine was a health hazard.

In a letter to the *Press-Gazette*, Bernard Lewis also pointed out that 14 percent of the margarine produced in the United States in 1943 was sent overseas to support the Allies while just 2.3 percent of butter was shipped.

"Someday dairy farmers will wake up and understand the truth of the complex butter-margarine controversies," Lewis wrote. "They will understand, as pointed out by the U.S. Bureau of Home Economics, that full production of margarine is needed in this country to insure an adequate dietary standard."

The margarine war would outlast World War II.

Under the mixed blessing category was the news that 120,000 of the 780,000 cigarettes purchased by residents of Green Bay and northeastern Wisconsin were set to be shipped from New York to soldiers overseas. The cigarettes were purchased from *Press-Gazette* carrier boys as part of a home front promotion to support the troops.

The officer overseeing the shipment informed the *Press-Gazette* that "there appears to be no saturation point for American cigarettes among our soldiers."

Muskrats and opossums weren't spared. Newman's on North Washington Street advertised its January clearance sale featuring blended muskrat furs as low as $189 and skunk-dyed opossum furs for $89.

And any anxiety among the residents along South Van Buren Street and Webster Avenue was soothed when they were told that their newspaper delivery was late only because their seventeen-year-old carrier boy, Frank Kunesh, was taking his Army Air Force examination. He passed, and the newspapers eventually found the front steps of the homes.

Women work on boat components at Algoma Plywoods in Algoma, Wisconsin, just east of Green Bay on Lake Michigan. (Photo courtesy of University of Wisconsin-Green Bay Archives)

***

(The following war updates were provided by Major John M. Walter in his role as the orientation and communications officer at Camp Wolters in Mineral Wells, Texas. He wrote the daily war updates for the base and included them in his personal diary.)

Jan. 1, 1944 - The invasion year has opened ... Soviet troops drive into Zhitomir and push on toward old Polish border ... it's one 35 miles away ... U.S. troops fighting in the streets of San Vittore, Italy, as Canadians push up Adriatic coast toward Pescara ... Battle of Cape Gloucester in New Britain seems to favor Marines, but progress is slow ... Hitler's New Year message to his people was pessimistic, as well as it may be ... American planes gave Paris a heavy pasting.

Jan. 13, 1944 - 43 Jap landing barges sunk between Saidor and Huon peninsula in New Guinea ... planes and PT boats did the trick ... huge U.S. raid on German plane centers cost us a record 64 planes, but was successful and further depleted the Axis supply of fighter planes ... Soviets capture Sarny in old Poland, start new offensive at Mozyr on central front, battle German counterattacks at Vinnitsa near Bug river, continue the advance at Kirovograd in the Dnieper bend ... Americans force Germans from Cirvaro in central Italy, are within four miles of Cassino.

Jan. 19, 1944 - Railroads are returned to their operators by the government, everyone gets a wage hike, and all presumably are happy. Another victory for labor union racketeers over the United States ... Soviets push through Nazi lines in north near Novgorod and Oranienbaum in move to clear Leningrad area ...Americans gain 1,000 yards from Japs in Arawe sector of New Britain ... Rapido river crossed by 5th Army troops driving on Cassino in central Italy.

Jan. 24, 1944 - Allied troops of 5th Army stream ashore along 80-mile strip south of Rome, meeting light resistance initially ... Germans on Cassino front appear to be thrown into wild confusion. There are demonstrations against the Nazis in occupied northern Italy ... Australians driving Japs from New Guinea strongholds in preparation for assault on Madang ... Soviets on Leningrad front within 5 miles of key rail junctions of Krasnogvardeisk and Tosno ... not much new from farther south.

Jan. 30, 1944 - Three thousand Allied planes hit Europe. 102 enemy fighters are shot down ... Frankfurt was involved, and the Templehof airport at Berlin is out of commission ... British troops are within 18 miles of Rome, and the Appian Way is cut ... Japan admits its base at Rabaul is doomed ... Soviets fall back in southern Ukraine east of Vinnitsa ... in the north, they clear the Leningrad-Moscow trunk rail line, and come within 23 miles of the Estonian border.

February 1944

"Spend, Sucker, Spend"

No sooner had the Brown County community finished relishing the news that its 1943 Christmas holiday sales were 26 percent higher than the previous year that it stared at a new challenge.

The country's fourth war bond drive put a $4,905,900 quota goal on Brown County, and the community had until Feb. 15 to get that much in donations and pledges in order to keep its wartime bond sale record perfect.

The bait was the Series E bonds that would mature in ten years and carry a 2.9 percent interest rate. To reach the quota was a badge of honor; to fall short was something no community wanted to try to justify.

The home front army was ready – more than 100 men and women volunteers were assigned to specific regions and municipalities of the county to solicit pledges from individuals. Another group focused on local industry. Another group contacted professional groups.

It wasn't designed to be a race, but it took on the semblance of one. Right away, the town of Suamico and village of Pulaski announced they reached their quotas. Soon, the town of Preble, the town of Lawrence, the town of Ashwaubenon, the town of Green Bay, the village of Denmark, and the city of De Pere got over the top.

Big ticket contributions came in from U.S. Steel and Montgomery Ward, whose mammoth purchases nationwide allowed Brown County to include some of those totals in its drive.

One woman appeared weekly to purchase bonds by using what she said were her husband's poker winnings. A hairdresser used her tips to buy bonds. A young girl said she gave up buying chewing gum in order to buy bonds.

But a week into the month, the county was far short of its goal. To increase sales, 1,800 tickets were made available for the premiere showing of the movie *What a Lady!* starring Rosalind Russell that would be shown at the Orpheum Theater. Each ticket purchased would also include a war bond.

Still, there was growing concern that the county wouldn't make it.

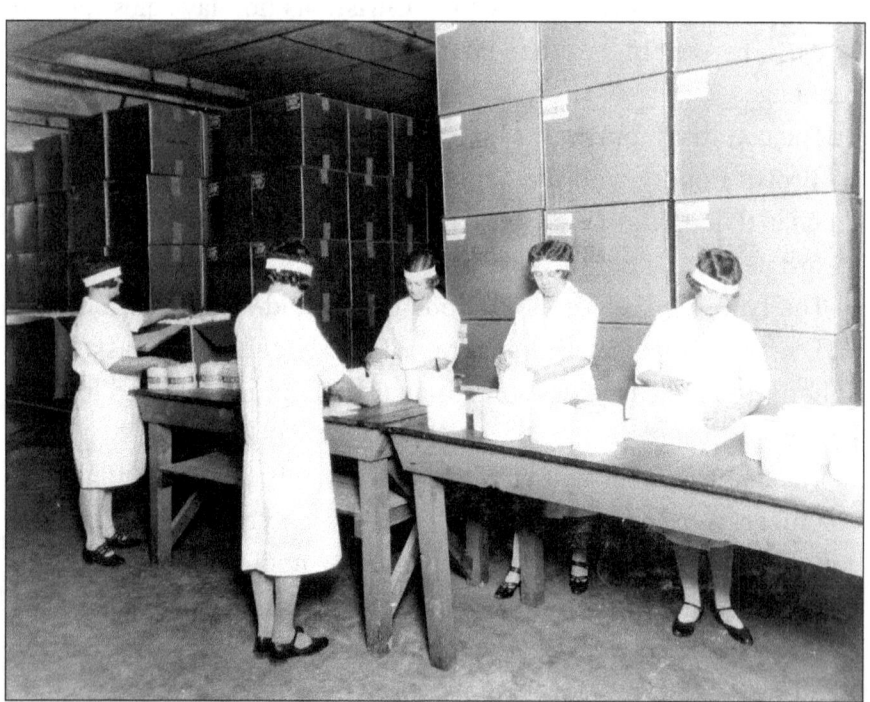

Women already were making up a growing percentage of the workforce when this photo was taken prior to the start of the war at Fort Howard Paper Company in Green Bay. (Photo courtesy of University of Wisconsin-Green Bay Archives)

Local News Highlights

February 1: The Swirl Beauty Shop, 113 N. Washington St., has February specials of a Super Oil Permanent for $2.95 and a Super Creme Wave for $4.

February 2: French crews were expected to arrive to man three PB sub-chasers built by the Leathem Smith Shipbuilding company in Sturgeon Bay.

February 7: City Councilman Dominic Olejniczak said he won't run for re-election in the 5th Ward in the spring election.

February 8: Injunctions were sought by the Office of Price Administration against the operators of the Carmen and Roxana hotels in Sturgeon Bay alleging they charged 25 cents to $1 in excess of the legal ceiling prices set by OPA.

February 11: There were 70 reported cases of chicken pox, 15 cases of scarlet fever, and seven cases each of measles and whooping cough in Green Bay in the month of January.

February 15: Two 15-year-old Green Bay boys confessed to running a stolen bicycle ring where they would confiscate bikes, dismantle them and use the parts for other stolen bikes so they weren't identifiable.

February 17: Fifteen no-decision bouts were staged by youngsters of the St. Patrick's parochial school and Sacred Heart of Manitowoc at the St. Patrick boxing ring.

February 28: West High School students began a house-to-house canvass west of the river to seek the names of West graduates in the service. East side families of West graduates are asked to mail the information to the school.

The drive chairmen, J.M. Conway and John Rose, pleaded with individuals to dip into their savings accounts.

"This can be done in view of the fact that deposits of all banks in the county are at the highest level in their history," they said. "If those with savings invest only a quarter in war bonds, we can go over the top on this drive as we did during previous drives."

Then organizers realized that residents of the town of Allouez had not been solicited door-to-door. The drive committee figured most residents worked in Green Bay and would have been tapped at their workplaces. So, on a snowy Saturday three days before the deadline, fifteen Boy Scouts went door-to-door and collected $4,000 in pledges.

The Oconto Brewing Company took out a full-page ad in the *Press-Gazette* that included large photographs of Hitler and Tojo with the challenge "They Haven't Quit Yet ... Have You?"

As the deadline neared, the drive committee eliminated the rule that limited volunteers to their assigned districts. Anyone could go anywhere to find people to make pledges.

The plea to invest in war bonds was most forceful in a full-page newspaper ad under the heading "Spend, Sucker, Spend" paid for by seventy-five of the community's businesses. It reminded people that financial prosperity was a façade, and buying bonds was the way to plan for the future.

The ad read: "Where's the money coming from? Prosperity? No ... war. From the business of death we've been forced into. From things made to kill people. From things made to kill other people so they won't kill us. There's no special Providence watching over this country, in spite of all our songs and slogans. Those War Bonds will guarantee your future, the financial future of you, your family, and the boys who are fighting for us all."

The day before the deadline, Conway and Rose said the goal was in sight. And when the sun rose on February 16, they were able to announce that the goal had been reached, and then some. Brown County had secured $5,476,200 in donations and pledges.

***

While the war bond committee was counting up the sales, thirteen sportswriters from throughout the country were casting their votes

Packers end Harry Jacunski catches a pass on the practice field. Jacunski played on the same Fordham University team as Vince Lombardi. The 1944 season would be his last full season with the Packers before transitioning to coaching in the college ranks.(Green Bay Press-Gazette photo)

for the NFL's most valuable player of 1943, an honor given to Don Hutson in 1941 and 1942.

This time, the award went to Chicago Bears quarterback Sid Luckman, who led his team to the '43 championship. He narrowly beat out Hutson, who set a season scoring record with 117 points.

Noteworthy was the fact that the Packers' Charley Brock, an offensive center who also played defense, finished fifth in the voting behind only Luckman, Hutson, the Redskins' Sammie Baugh, and Giants halfback Ward Cuff, who would play for the Packers three years later.

The military and Packers football crossed paths when Lt. Milt Gantenbein, the former Packers end, met Lt. Commander George Halas while they were both stationed at the Naval Air Technical Training Center in Lawton, Oklahoma. In fact, when Halas was being transferred to San Diego awaiting his next assignment, several officers gave him a going-away gift, a $150 watch, and Gantenbein presented the watch to his former rival.

Packers president Lee Joannes received a letter from T-Sgt. Norbert Cuene of De Pere, stationed in London, who needed to settle a bet with a Minnesota soldier over Packer Andy Uram's weight. Cuene won the bet.

Elmer Layden
NFL commissioner

The Packers were in the process of deciding who would join Lambeau's coaching staff in the wake of the December resignation of long-time line coach Richard "Red" Smith, who was on the verge of joining the staff of the New York Giants. Lambeau said he had twelve applicants for the part-time position, many of whom he termed as well-known names in national football circles.

"Coaching work in the league is much more detailed than it was years ago, necessitating a division of labor to cover every department of play," Lambeau said.

Hutson's coaching job was to be year-round. He was assigned the task of studying scouting reports and drawing up opponents' plays on cards to be distributed to Packer players. He would help coach the ends, too.

There was a stir mid-month when Bob Carpenter, the new owner of baseball's Philadelphia Phillies, convinced the owners of the eight American Association Midwest Class A baseball teams – one of which was the Milwaukee Brewers – to approach NFL commissioner Elmer Layden with the idea of creating minor league football teams. The idea was to have each of the minor league baseball teams form their own football team and use the playing field, grandstands, labor and concessions that otherwise would remain idle once baseball shut down for the season.

Lambeau had a one-word response to the idea. He called it nonsense since all pro teams were struggling to recruit enough players during the war. Lambeau was also opposed to adding new NFL franchises for the 1944 season for the same reason.

"I'm not against granting of good franchises, but I don't think new clubs should operate until conditions warrant such a move," Lambeau said. "I feel that the old standbys (the Packers and other veteran teams) can replace their losses to the armed services because they have a nucleus to start with, but I doubt that a new club can come in cold and build a football squad from the ground up and sustain caliber.

"We've lost three men already and perhaps another half dozen will be gone before the season opens," Lambeau continued. "We're scouring the country for replacements and we find that the prospects are decidedly limited. College players, unless they're 4-F (not qualified for service), are unavailable, and prospects from other sources are slim. Honorable discharges are our best bet at this point."

Lambeau continued to defend players who weren't healthy enough for the military, but could play pro football.

"The army can't tape up a weak knee or give a boy a few minutes on the bench when he gets tired," he said. "Why, we've had a lot of players who can't walk ten miles."

Meanwhile, Arthur Bouffard, rehabilitation director at the Green Bay Vocational School, said 25 to 30 percent of the servicemen returning from the war will be classed as "mental cases."

Packers fans took note when Chicago Bears football legend Bronko Nagurski, who retired as a player after the 1943 season, took his pre-induction army physical at Fort Snelling, Minnesota.

***

People found ways to keep informed and to be entertained.

Two motion pictures were shown at the YMCA, preceded by a war reel *Victory in Sicily*. Then, four members of the Hi-Y Club conducted a worship service.

Fifty-four tables of bridge were played at card parties sponsored by members of the auxiliary to St. Mary's Mothers and Infants home.

And the latest jitterbug steps were taught at the Allouez Community House on Saturday evenings.

***

The voices from the *Press-Gazette* editorial page continued to carry patriotic tones, but with an undertone of politics.

This Is Our Real Foe
February 2, 1944

When suffering of children or the helpless is depicted on the screen many in the audience turn away or close their eyes. Something hurts them inside when anguish is visited upon others. They will probably turn the page rather than read the details of the beastly horror heaped upon American boys in the hands of slant-eyed savages of Japan.

But that story should be required reading for every American because this war bids fair to stretch out for many years and its most hideous crimes are as yet uncommitted, dreadful as that idea may appear.

Cracking Down on Drunks at the Wheel
February 2, 1944

It is at once reassuring and alarming to read the bulletin of the state motor vehicle department that during the year just passed 3,029 drivers in Wisconsin lost their driving licenses upon conviction for driving a motor vehicle while drunk.

It is reassuring because it shows alert enforcement attitudes by Wisconsin officers. It is alarming because it demonstrates the huge educational job that remains in the field of traffic safety.

On Lincoln's Birthday
February 12, 1944

We think that if Mr. Lincoln were here today he would support every practical means of collecting the terrible power of America into one instrument of violence with which to strike the foe down mortally wounded.

Rev. Ben C. Plopper (from left) and local Sea Scouts (B.S.A.) representative Harold Miracle present certificates to new Eagle Scouts Robert Wood and James VanCaster on February 23, 1944. (Green Bay Press-Gazette photo)

Some Make Wars and Some Fight Them
February 16, 1944

Senator Henry Cabot Lodge, 41, of Massachusetts has resigned his seat in Congress to take the field. He asked the War department for "combat service." When put to the test the senator never hesitated. His decision reflects heavily on some ardent New Dealers who had a big part in getting the country into the war, but have since been racing up alleys, simulating limps and forcing tubercular coughs to avoid the only honorable course open to them to resigning their seats and taking on the uniform.

Religious Edifices in War
February 21, 1944

The fact that prominent prelates of the Catholic church rushed to assure the American people that our shelling of the monastery on Mt.

Military personnel man the sweet corn machines in the Larsen Canning Company plant in Green Bay. (Photo courtesy of University of Wisconsin-Green Bay Archives)

Cassino was proper and not to be resented is a caliper measurement of the density of ignorance of our people respecting the practices of armies. Probably these statements were suggested by the Washington authorities.

***

(The following war updates were provided by Major John M. Walter in his role as the orientation and communications officer at Camp Wolters in Mineral Wells, Texas. He wrote the daily war updates for the base and included them in his personal diary.)

Feb. 2, 1944 - U.S. forces landed at two points on Kwajalein atoll in the Marshalls Jan 31 ... there's a tough job ahead in this one ... Soviet Union sets up 16 Russian republics, each with its own army and government of foreign affairs ... looks a shade like the British commonwealth, but will bear more study ... Reds capture Kingisepp, and reach pre-war Estonian town of Keikimo, 7 miles northeast of Narva ... they have captured Novinka on the Leningrad-Vitebsk line ... Allies are in the outskirts of Campoleone, 16 miles southeast of Rome ... within half a mile of Cisterna, guarding the Appian Way 24 miles from Rome.

Feb. 7, 1944 - Elite SS troops counterattack south of Rome, forcing British back 2 miles ... Cassino now is virtually surrounded ... Helsinki bombed by Soviets in drive to knock the Finns out of the war ... 75,000 Nazis trapped in Dnieper bend near Nikopol, and 100,000 more are in trouble near Smela ... in old Poland the Soviets take Mizoch, 55 miles from the Odessa-Warsaw railway, and Mlininov, 30 miles southwest of Rovno and 82 miles from Low ... Three more islands in Kwalalein atoll fall to Americans.

Feb. 11, 1944 - Nazi drive against the Rome beachhead is slowed down, largely by Allied concentrations of artillery ... U.S., Australian forces unite near Saidor in New Guinea, completing occupation of the Huon peninsula ... U.S. bombers hit Brunswick, Germany, and Gilze-Rijen, Holland ... 84 Nazi planes shot down ... Soviets hasten doom of Germans trapped in Ukraine ... gain 6 more miles near Korsun ... to southeast, Gen. Malinovsky is outflanking Krivoi Rog, big iron center ... in the north, Reds are 7 miles from Luga on Leningrad-Pskov rail line ... air raid on Riga, Lett capital, announced from Stockholm ... Greek guerrilla bands sign truce.

Feb. 15, 1944 - Reds take Korsun in Ukraine trap ... Nazis drive wedge into Dnieper river ring in the north, driving south between Lake Peipus and Luga, Soviet spearheads are 40 miles from Pskov ... British night bombers siren then air power over Anzio-Nettuno ... Allied beachhead substantially unchanged over the weekend ... Weary Americans gain 200 yards in Cassino ... they have started shelling the monastery where the Benedictine order was founded in 529 A.D. ... Americans occupy Rooke island between New Guinea and New Britain.

Feb. 22, 1944 - Red army breaks into Krivoi Rog in offensive against Axis forces east of the Bug ... 3-sided drive on Pskov continues. They're only 28 miles away on north ... 5,000 bombers pounded Germany for the last 36 hours ... Allies at Anzio block weakened German blows, with bloody losses for enemy ... Last Japs being cleared from Eniwetok in Marshalls ... Tokyo announces its chiefs of Army and Navy general staffs have been ousted.

Feb. 28, 1944 - Red bombers devastate Helsinki with 600 planes for 12 hours ... Great U.S. invasion convoy arrives safely in England ... Japs meet reverses from Burma to Rabaul ... 23 ships were sunk, a revised figure, in the Feb. 16-17 raid on Truk ... Jap air force is believed depleted ... Red army overruns German reinforcements north and northwest of Pskov ... 5th Army at Cassino repels two light German attacks.

March 1944

Victory Farms

As the war got older, the workforce at home got younger. Plans were underway to enroll, train and place high school boys and girls on Brown County farms in the coming summer. They would be called Victory Farm Volunteers and the program would be supported by federal funds. The youths would have to be at least fourteen years old, willing to do the farm work, and have parental permission.

At the same time, the faculties at the three Green Bay high schools began filling out psychological questionnaires for all students who would be going into the armed services. This was being done at the request of Selective Service to help it identify any potential mental problems prior to induction. Mental stress led to the discharge of more than 100,000 men in 1943.

And students at the junior high schools were busy creating game materials, ash trays, writing tablets and other items that would be sent to the country's veterans hospitals.

The social problems class at West High School conducted a poll of teachers, local managers, railroad workers and other adults asking opinions on the chance for world peace after the war. Nine thought it was probable, thirty thought it was possible, and two thought it impossible.

Asked if eighteen-year-olds should be allowed to vote, 101 students said yes and 39 said no.

A free evening training class in industrial psychology was set to be taught at Washington Junior High School. It was intended primarily for those in executive capacities in war industries and for young women interested in supervisory industrial jobs.

Boy Scouts continued to be visible on the home front. A major city-wide newspaper, magazine and waste paper collection, all tied in bundles and put at the curb, was picked up by the scouts riding with city truck drivers.

Youth weren't eligible for many jobs, but future employment looked possible for those who wanted a career in shipbuilding. Leathem Smith Shipbuilders in Sturgeon Bay, in great need of welders because of the wartime manpower shortage, was ready to train inexperienced employees. It paid 75 cents an hour during the training, and as soon as the worker passed the required navy tests, the pay would increase. The company also promised regular employment in the post-war era.

The city's Association of Commerce (the predecessor to today's Chamber of Commerce) was promoting a promising employment picture for Green Bay when the war ended. The fact that the city wasn't the center of a booming war industry would mean that major postwar adjustments and reconversions wouldn't be required.

C.R. Phenicie, chairman of the association's employment committee, said employment in Green Bay would be a sure thing after the war for returning servicemen and women.

"Some people criticize Green Bay for not having a booming war industry," Phenicie said. "But I say we are not always at war and we are better off as we are. Our stability of location, population and industry will make our city prosperous. War inflation means postwar deflation. Jobs in war towns will decrease in proportion to the amount they grew during the war. A lot of towns – some of them not far from Green Bay – are going to be fooled about this."

The community took a lasting step to honor one of its fallen heroes. The Green Bay post of the American Legion voted to change its

Local News Highlights

March 7: The East High School class of 1919, which had to cancel its school play because of World War I, cancelled its 25th reunion because the current war made transportation too difficult.

March 17: More than 700 fans attended the boxing match between students at the De Pere and St. Norbert high schools held at De Pere's gymnasium.

March 23: The Krambo Food Stores were selling butter for 44 cents a pound, a box of corn flakes for a nickel and a 100-pound sack of potatoes for $1.59.

March 31: The Rev. Francis Rose, superintendent of the St. Joseph's Orphanage, asked for public cooperation to prevent the introduction of measles and other communicable diseases at the facility. He said there were no measles cases at the orphanage, but if a single case is diagnosed, all children will have to be quarantined and that will mean they'll miss out of upcoming Easter events. *(Green Bay Press-Gazette photo)*

name to the Sullivan-Wallen post, honoring Earl Wallen, a West High graduate and US Marines veteran who died of wounds suffered in the Japanese attack on Pearl Harbor.

The local Marine Corps recruiter said the corps was now available to men between the ages of thirty-eight and forty-five for guard duty at navy yards and other shore stations in the country. Minor physical defects would be tolerated.

Some advertising had a wartime subtlety. Calvert Whiskey warned its buyers and drinkers against loose talk. "War information is strictly secret unless you see it printed or hear it broadcast," the ad read. "It shouldn't be told – even confidentially. Keep it quiet, to keep it safe."

And the ad for weight loss supplement Marmola was under the headline "Girdle Shortage Need Not Worry Certain Fat Women."

Traveling got complicated for some Green Bay-area residents as winter neared its end. Rationing boards refused to allow sufficient gasoline for many who spent part of the winter in Florida, so they had to get in line for railroad tickets in order to get home.

Johnny (Blood) McNally
(Green Bay Press-Gazette photo)

***

The paths of the 1944 Packers and the world war continued to intersect, although some were lodged in past Packers history and the characters who labored then.

Lambeau, visiting in New York, sat down with *The New York*

Times's Arthur Daley to share a letter he received from former Packer Johnny Blood, who was working with a bombing unit in India. Blood wrote that his immediate ambition was to learn how to operate a bomber and go for a ride someday.

"From long experience, I'm fully aware of how his mind works," Lambeau said. "Mark this well. Someday, Johnny is going to borrow a bomber and bomb Tokyo by himself. It would be typical of him.

"Years ago, when he was playing football for me on the Packers, he used to say, 'I want a sensational life and a sensational finish.' If you read of a lone raider over Japan, it will be Johnny Blood."

NFL communications director George Strickler sent some requested football statistics to Blood in China and received the following reply, which probably made more sense at the time:

> "Dear Scribbler. China is a better hole at end of line. Received letter, dope and Paulette Goddard same day. Got football broadcasts on super pro receiver. We called it Don Hutson. Thank you for the dope. Thank Hutson for Lambeau. Thank God for Uncle Sam. Thank your stars this is not collect. (Signed) John J. McNally"

Lambeau was more concerned about the makeup of his 1944 team. He would learn days later that veteran Andy Uram, who still held the NFL record for the longest run from scrimmage (97 yards), passed his physical to be inducted into the navy and would report in thirty days. Uram had been exempt from the draft because he was already a father at the time of Pearl Harbor, but the draft board reclassified him 1-A because he was in a non-essential industry. Uram would eventually serve in the South Pacific, but sustained foot problems that prevented him from playing football after the war.

Three other Packers from the 1943 team were now in the armed services. Tony Canadeo was stationed at an army base in Texas, Dick Evans joined the marines, and Chet Adams was with the military police.

Lambeau predicted there would be more Packers players joining the service before the 1944 season. It was one reason he continued to favor the practice of pro teams combining their rosters for the '44 season or for as long as the war continued.

Lambeau was preparing for the annual league meeting of owners in April, where he planned to recommend a rules change. He wanted to preserve the excitement of the kickoff return by penalizing teams that kicked off out of bounds. Lambeau's plan was to have the kicking team penalized, but be forced to kick again so there would still be a return. As many times as they kicked it out of bounds, they would be penalized until there was a return.

One event that Lambeau did not attend was a farewell party for former Packers line coach Richard (Red) Smith at the Elks Lodge. Smith had just been named an assistant coach of the New York Giants and the circumstances of his December resignation from the Packers weren't disclosed.

Interestingly, Smith received a gift of a hunting jacket from Elks exalted ruler Dominic Olejniczak, who would later become the long-time president of the Packers. And the speaker at the party was Charlie Grimm, the former and future manager of the Chicago Cubs and future manager of the Milwaukee Braves.

Hutson continued to pile up honors. His forty-seven pass receptions in 1943 was far more than any other player and the 237 receiving yards he totaled against Brooklyn in '43 was a record.

***

Green Bay Press-Gazette editorial page opinions continued to pass before readers eyes.

Intolerance - Humanity's Special Poison
March 6, 1944

There is a movement or at least a disposition, to treat the period from Lincoln's birthday to Washington's as one for the application of remedies, tonics and antidotes against perhaps the greatest curse the human race has known – intolerance of race, creed, color or class. A man's face and color are beyond his control. That one person, upon this earth for a short spell, should curl back his lips at another like a canine because that other has hair of a different hue or eyes of dissimilar tint is assuredly one of the strongest links that scientists could submit to establish that we are descended from the lower animals and not so far distant from them as we had hoped.

The Governor Organizes an Aviation Board
March 11, 1944

Governor Goodland has acted wisely in taking steps to create an advisory aeronautics board to assist the Wisconsin Public Service Commission and the Wisconsin State Planning Board in anticipating and solving the problems that will come with the expansion of commercial aviation in Wisconsin after the war.

Russian Foreign Policy
March 15, 1944

The Canadians have turned out a film under the above title which is showing in this country with the evident purpose of quieting fears that are general respecting the course of the Soviets in the future and after the Axis is sprawled upon the ground.

Our attitude toward such endeavors should be open and friendly, but not careless or confiding. We must realize that the hopes and plans for future world peace cannot mature without a mutual trust.

Capt. McCarthy is the Type
March 21, 1944

Capt. Joseph McCarthy is the type impregnated with the mother wit and quick, penetrating ability gloved in prudence that has already redeemed the Republican party in most of the country and bids fair to rescue the nation from those who are still dizzied by subterfuge and dazzled by sophistry.

Tony Walter

Our Army and Its Work
March 25, 1944

Occupational deferments are to melt and disappear under the latest Roosevelt order. The nation and its industries will just have to look after themselves as youth everywhere is swept into the armed forces. Much can be said in favor of this new ruling. More might be said were the President to take the people into his confidence and reveal to them what is expected of our armed forces in addition to the clean-up program now underway in the Pacific. All we need is what the enemy knows already.

***

(The following war updates were provided by Major John M. Walter in his role as the orientation and communications officer at Camp Wolters in Mineral Wells, Texas. He wrote the daily war updates for the base and included them in his personal diary.)

March 3, 1944 - Lt. Gen. Clark says Anzio-Nettuno beachhead now is safe ... Allies set to repel any Nazi blows ... Americans on Los Negros are heavily reinforced ... U.S. bombers hit French, German areas ... Soviets outflank Nazis at Narva, and near Ostrov, south of Pskov.

March 7, 1944 - 850 American bombers rake Berlin ... they dropped more than 2,000 tons of bombs, and the raid was hailed as a success, but we lost 68 bombers and 700 trained men ... 83 German fighters were knocked down ... Reds cut Odessa-Lwow rail line but taking Volochisk ... Marshall Zhukov's men did the trick ... Americans continue advance on Los Negros in Solomons ... Losses of Nazis at Anzio may have weakened their invasion defenses.

March 10, 1944 - Collapse of Jap position in Admiralty islands threatened as American warships steam into Seadler harbor ... Jap planes stage counterattack on Eniwetok atoll in Marshalls ... Marines advancing in northern New Britain toward Talasea airstrip ... General Alexander says Anzio beachhead situation is improved ... Stockholm reports that Berlin 'has ceased to be a capital or even a town' as heavy Allied raids continue, drawing few German fighter planes ... Soviets breach German lines in drive toward Black Sea ports of Nikolsev and Kherson ... they are 55 miles above the former.

March 14, 1944 - With the Germans wiped out at Kherson, the Soviets swing northwestward toward Nikolaev, the next objective ... there is fighting in Tarnopol, to the west ... France hit by three Allied raids in one day ... Soviet Union gives Finns more time to consider peace proposal ... Cornered Japs on Bougainville attack, 1,000 being killed by Americans ... Weather conditions bring war in Italy to standstill.

March 17, 1944 - American amphibious forces invade Manus island, largest of the Admiralty group in the Southwest Pacific, and land-based Liberators make their first raid on Truk ... new air successes are reported over Truk, Weak and Rabaul ... Soviet army cuts Odessa-Zhmerinka railway, sealing off Black Sea port of Nikolaev, the capture of which is believed imminent ... Marshal Kong's 2nd Army has reached the Bessarabian frontier along the Bug river ... U.S. fighters down 76 planes in big battle over Europe ... Allies occupy three-fourths of Cassino, mop up Germans in pockets of resistance.

March 19, 1944 - Routing the Nazi 6th Army, the Soviets complete an 11-day battle near Nikolaev, and the Red 2nd Army has broken through to the Bessarabian border on the Dniester river ... U.S. drops bombs on Matsuwa island, 960 miles from Tokyo in the north ... Paramushiro in the Kuriles was attacked twice ... RAF follows up U.S. AAF blow at South Germany with raid on Frankfurt ... U.S. troops take main Jap base of Lorengau in the Admiralty islands.

March 23, 1944 - Allied soldiers, using everything from flame throwers to bush knives, advance slowly in battle for Cassino ... Jap destroyer and two cargo ships sunk off New Guinea ... U.S. bombers unopposed over Rabaul ... 600 AAF bombers hit Berlin by daylight, as RAF follows up with strong smash at Frankfurt ... 38,000 air trainees will be released to the ground forces ... Nazis order mobilization of southeast Europe against the Soviet advance ... Reds are eight miles from Nikolaev on the Bug estuary ... they have reached Kowel inside old Poland and made further gains in the Tarnopol region, up to 30 miles.

March 27, 1944 - After an historic 800-mile march from Stalingrad, the Red Army has reached the Prut river frontier of Rumania, from which Hitler launched his 1941 invasion ... Kong's 2nd Army emerged on the banks of the Prut along a 53-mile front ... 300 Japs were killed in renewal of their hopeless assaults on Bougainville island ... Wake island is bombed again ... A major battle is developing in the Chindwin river country of northern Burma, where three Jap invasion columns are engaged in bloody fighting with the Allies ... Nothing new as Cassino struggle continues ... Churchill confidently predicts victory, says war against Japan may be won sooner than expected ... Allied bombers pound French coastal area from Calais to Cherbourg.

March 31, 1944 - Palau island, 460 miles east of the Philippines, is attacked by Admiral Nimitz' Pacific fleet ... U.S. land-based bombers hit Truk for first time, destroying 59 planes on the ground ... All eastern Rumania has been outflanked by the Soviets ... with Czernowitz captured, the Reds have begun their invasion of the Balkans, aimed at stripping Germany of her oil reserves ... the Soviets also are hitting hard between Czernowitz and Lwow ... Sofia rail yards bombed by 15th AAF as RAF goes over western Germany.

April 1944

Expand?

Coping with the war was the biggest challenge for NFL owners as they tried to adjust to the manpower limitations while still keeping their game in play. But there was pressure from some circles to require the league to cease operations until the war ended.

"The league objective is getting the war over as quickly as possible," Commissioner Elmer Layden said when the league meeting convened in Philadelphia eighteen days into April. "Therefore, it is up to the government. Whenever they want us to quit we are ready. But I feel we are making a definite contribution to the wartime athletic program by keeping the league in operation. The game is an incentive to our American kids, who gain a fighting spirit that serves them well in war or peace."

Layden waffled on the issue of using young boys to play pro football.

"I think boys of sixteen or seventeen should definitely be in college first," he said. "We must consider the boy himself and his development. However, it may be necessary to use some of the younger players due to the manpower shortage. We are exploring many sources of material."

League bylaws had stipulated that no player may compete in the NFL until the class in which he first entered college as a freshman was graduated. But team owners agreed in 1943 to let teams use college juniors and seniors returning from the service as long as their college had abandoned football.

Although team owners remained committed to the continuation of the league under the limited player circumstances, there was uncertainty about the number of teams that would take the field in 1944. Some believed that the league should proceed with the same eight teams that competed in 1943. But there was support for boosting the total to ten or eleven teams, with the Boston Yanks and Cleveland Rams being active members, and the Eagles and Steelers ending their one-year experiment as a merged team.

When the votes were counted in Philly, the league went with eleven teams with the Eagles functioning as a "roving" team that would compete against teams from both the east and west divisions. Then, Art Rooney and Bert Bell of the Steelers met with Charley Bidwell of the Chicago Cardinals and decided to merge into one team for the '44 season, making it a 10-team league.

Expansion after the war seemed to be a given by this time.

Guy Butler, writing for *The Miami News,* wrote that a larger NFL was inevitable.

"All the experts assure us that sports are in for an unprecedented boom after the unpleasantness is finished and Hitler is strung up from yon sour apple tree," he wrote. "Who will own franchises? Will we have a National League, in fact ... with San Francisco, Los Angeles, Miami, Dallas and all other cities scattered from here to yonder on the North American map included?

"Frankly, the whole kaboodle can't be accommodated. New York and Boston and Philadelphia and Chicago and Pittsburgh and Cleveland and Washington and Detroit and Green Bay cannot be left out. They're big cities (except Green Bay, which is a great draw.)"

The handful of hopeful team owners who submitted applications for franchises were refunded their $25,000 application fee and told to bide their time until after the war.

These included men such as Abe Watner in Baltimore, Sam Cor-

> ## Local News Highlights
>
> **April 4:** All Green Bay area retail stores, city and county offices, the library and museum will close for several hours Good Friday afternoon so employees can attend church services.
>
> **April 7:** Vandals caused damage to the shelter at Fisk Park, with officials estimating the damage at $14.90. Better police surveillance was proposed.
>
> **April 13:** For the second time, Press-Gazette carrier boy Bernard Jones sold the most war bonds and stamps on his delivery beat, This time he sold $9,115 to his customers.
>
> **April 15:** Counterfeit gasoline stamps have been passed by motorists in several cities in the Green Bay area. Officials said many of the fake stamps were passed by out-of-state motorists.
>
> **April 19:** A vicious-looking set of false teeth carved from ivory and said to be just like a set George Washington used may be seen in the medical display at the Neville Public Museum.
>
> **April 25:** Midwest Airways files an application with the Civil Aeronautics Board for permission to provide air service from Milwaukee to Marquette, Michigan, with stops in Fond du Lac, Oshkosh, Appleton, Green Bay, Marinette and Escanaba.

davana in Buffalo, and Ernie Nevers and Anthony Morabito in San Francisco.

Prior to conducting their annual draft, the owners voted for a one-year trial to allow coaches to coach on the sidelines. Up to that point, coaches were forbidden from actually coaching from the sidelines during games. The new rule gave them permission as long as they stayed within a ten-yard space near the bench. They also decided that players could come to the sidelines for coaching during a timeout, which had been forbidden.

The player draft was conducted with the knowledge that of the 300 players drafted in 1943, only twenty-three ever reported to a team

Even plays staged for publicity photos could get rather physical, as evidenced by this 1941 helmetless shot of star running back Tony Canadeo (3) dashing through a hole in the line created in part by blocking back Larry Buhler (52). Linebacker Frank Balazs (35) is about to take the brunt of Buhler's block. (Green Bay Press-Gazette photo)

practice. It was just assumed that the majority of the players coming out of college would be entering the armed forces.

There were some notable names that appeared in the 1944 draft. Wisconsin's Pat Harder was chosen by the Chicago Cardinals and Northwestern quarterback Otto Graham was picked by the Detroit Lions.

Only one of the thirty players selected by Lambeau in 1944 appeared on any Packers roster. (Merv Pregulman would play in 1946.) One of his picks was former Illinois and Purdue lineman Alex Agase, whose future in pro football would be with the Cleveland Browns before he became head coach at Northwestern.

The league schedule showed the Packers with five home games and five road games, but Lambeau didn't say if any of the home games would be played in Milwaukee.

Also coming out of the league meeting were reports that Hutson might decide to play another season. And there was speculation that Jim Crowley would become head coach of the Boston franchise after the war.

There was finally a Green Bay sighting of Babe Webb, the halfback from Texas who initially signed with the Packers in 1941 and 1942, but was unable to book transport out of Hawaii where he was coaching a high school team.

He finally got on a boat in October 1943, returned to Texas and got married, then came to Green Bay six months later to meet Lambeau.

***

Opinions were offered daily in the *Green Bay Press-Gazette,* and the April 18 editorial called out those who would punish Japanese Americans who remain loyal to the United States.

"This country is yet to face out on the Pacific coast its most severe trial in resisting the warp and twist of racial resentment led by war's embittered poisons," led the editorial under the heading "Test in Intolerance."

"For every class there seems to be represented in the shouting that the man of Jap blood must go ... Hundreds of these Jap-Americans are buried in our Army cemeteries in Italy. Thousands of them are preparing to face the steel and fire that is battle.

"The keystone of America's arch will drop from place if we ever permit ourselves to single out faithful and well-behaved citizens for reprisals because of acts beyond their power to prevent and committed by others."

Other opinions:

An Opportunity Awaits
April 3, 1944

The fact that 1944 is an election year may be the most promising harbinger for the future of America of anything in sight if the people will arise to the solemnity of the occasion. Tomorrow men and women of Wisconsin will register their opinion of the most suitable candidate for the Republican nomination for the presidency that through him they may assert again their abiding faith in the institutions of liberty and cleave to a policy at one, proud, manly and intelligent.

As the Asian War Years Stretch Ahead
April 11, 1944

We have now moved onto the continent of Asia, the greatest and least understood of all continents. As its vast areas become dotted with the bleached bones of American youth and it thirstily drinks up their blood, the folks back home will want a running story of information about that may be denied because ion newsprint scarcity.

The trouble with the world is that it is too big. But for some reason God made it that way.

Trout at Risk
April 17, 1944

Possibly excepting Green Bay Packer football fans, there is no more devoted class of sports lovers in Wisconsin than that large although uncounted fraternity that derives soulful satisfaction out of casting a fly or dunking live bait in pursuit of that aristocrat of Wisconsin inland fishing – the trout. In this community and in many others, however, there has been a tacit realization and recognition that trout fishing in Wisconsin has deteriorated and that artificial propagation and planting alone have not succeeded in heading off the deterioration.

Sins of Censorship
April 24, 1944

Probably the biggest piece of blown-up blubber the war has produced is the censorship. Proclaimed as an effort to prevent the enemy from obtaining information to his advantage, it is employed primarily to gum the eyes and pack the ears of the home folks upon the theory that they will be driven easier if kept ignorant.

***

The month brought the 1944 presidential election to the forefront, and Wisconsin was poised to play a significant role in the Republican Party's choice of a candidate. The 1940 nominee, Wendell Willkie, decided to use the Wisconsin presidential preference primary election as a possible launching pad for his candidacy and campaigned heavily in the state in the days leading up to the vote.

There were other names of note seeking delegates in the election – New York Gov. Thomas Dewey, former Minnesota Gov. Harold Stassen, and General Douglas MacArthur – although none had actually declared his candidacy.

MacArthur issued a statement to indicate that he was not seeking the Republican nomination, but hinted that he would accept it if drafted by the convention.

The vote sealed Willkie's fate as he finished far behind the other three names. One day after the election, Willkie announced he was ending his campaign.

Then, his health deteriorated, impacted by his lifetime of smoking and increased drinking. A series of heart attacks eventually put him in a New York hospital and a throat infection led to his decline. Willkie died a week into October at the age of fifty-two.

The Democrats were waiting for Roosevelt to say if he would seek a fourth term. The party's Brown County chairman, attorney G.F. Clifford, said the elimination of Willkie removed the only GOP candidate with any liberal ideas. He said the different factions of the Democratic Party would cooperate to back FDR.

***

It was a month of firsts.

A new traveling x-ray unit to be used at fifty Green Bay industries was designed to catch undiscovered tuberculosis stages of employees. It was sponsored by the state board of health.

The largest locomotives to ever come to Green Bay arrived from Chicago as part of the Milwaukee Road line. The engines, ninety-four feet long, marked the first time that passenger trains powered by steam ran from Chicago to Green Bay without making a change en route.

German prisoners of war worked in the Door County fruit orchards during the spring. (Green Bay Press-Gazette photo)

And the first meeting of a new state aeronautics board was held to discuss specific steps in the expansion of airports and aviation training after the war. Gov. Walter Goodland said that aviation in the future might parallel the phenomenal growth of motor vehicle transport.

It was also pointed out that thousands of Wisconsin men who have learned to fly in their military service will want to fly when they return to civilian life.

***

(The following war updates were provided by Major John M. Walter in his role as the orientation and communications officer at Camp Wolters in Mineral Wells, Texas. He wrote the daily war updates for the base and included them in his personal diary.)

April 2, 1944 - Milder peace terms have been offered the Finns by the Soviet Union, and a decision is expected Monday ... Reds have fought their way into Khotin to block the last escape route of Germans in the Kamenets-Podolsk pocket ... they have reached the Tatar pass leading through the Carpathian mountains to Czechoslovakia ... American planes bomb Schaffhausen in Switzerland by mistake, killing 27 ... Japs are within 16 miles of Allied base at Imphal in northeastern India ... Truk bombed for fifth time in three days ... Capture of Mount Marrone above Cassino in Italy by 5th Army troops has partially straightened the line in that sector.

April 6, 1944 - Twenty-seven years ago today, the United States declared war on Germany ... 18 months later Germany sued for peace ... Italians fighting with Allies defend Mount Marrone against German counterattacks... American bombers pound Weak in New Guinea ... Japs drive deeper into the Imphal plain in their invasion of India ... The Soviet Black Sea fleet is in control of the Odessa escape route as the Reds near outskirts of the city ... More British coastal territory restricted for invasion purposes ... Rumania's great oil fields are plastered by Allied bombers.

April 10, 1944 - U.S. will make no negotiated peace with Germany or Japan, says Secretary of State Hull ... American bombers dropped 386 tons of bombs on enemy bases in Bismarck sea area ... Hollandia took the biggest rap ... Iasi is virtually encircled by Soviets in Rumania ... other Red units are in freight yards of Odessa ... Large fleets of American heavy bombers strike airplane factories in Poland, East Prussia, northeast Germany.

April 14, 1944 - U.S. and Britain have called for showdown with Sweden on matter of supplying Nazis with war materials ... Kuban Cossacks of 4th Ukrainian Army are sweeping through low valleys only 25 miles north of Sevastopol ... Axis troops are driven across Dniester river west of Odessa as Reds recapture Ovidiopol ... Action by patrols in Garigliano valley is only news from Italy ... 3,000 Allied planes swarm over Germany, costing the Nazis 134 planes ... American losses were 48 heavy bombers and 10 fighters ... More than 200 Allied planes attack Hollandia in Dutch New Guinea.

April 20, 1944 - Adolf Hitler is 55 years old today. May it be his last birthday ... in the past 30 hours, bombs have been dropped on Germany and Nazi-held territory at rate of 300 tons every hour ... there were 6,000 flights yesterday ... Germans have launched large scale attack before Lwow in old Poland ... battle for Sevastopol is becoming more like a siege ... British relief column has broken through to Kohima in India ... Lt. Col. Tommy Hitchcock, famous polo player, killed in English plane crash ... Four sharp German attacks against Anzio beachhead repulsed by Allies.

April 26, 1944 - Russians say they shall pursue the Nazis "onto the soil of Germany itself" ... Gen. George Patton, an unqualified and irresponsible officer, speaking in England, says that "after the war Britain and America will rule the world" ... hate to think what would happen if Soviet Marshal Zhukov said something like that about Russia ... Hitler inspects the Atlantic wall ... Ujelong, westernmost still of the Marshalls, mopped up by Americans ... Pincers tighten on two Jap-held airfields near Hollandia in Dutch New Guinea ...Allies already are flying out of recently captured Aitape field ... Metz, Nancy and Dijon are among principal European targets in another day of heavy air blows, tuning up for the invasion.

April 29, 1944 - Allied assaults over Germany reach new peak in 15th day, and invasion seems very near now ... French coastal area receives worst pounding ... Frank Knox, 70, secretary of the Navy, dies of heart attack ... Japs are losing ground on widely scattered fronts ... they have taken a complete whipping in New Guinea, have been thrown back from their Honan objectives in China, are pinned down before Kohima and Imphal in India, and are being slapped around by Stillwell's infantry in Burma ... what price oriental invincibility now? ... Soviet air force attacks Lwow in strength ... Germans claim Soviet attacks against Sevastopol have failed ... Berlin announces its anti-invasion command is ready for anything ... and will get it, too.

May 1944

An Essential Difference

With the war intensity at a peak and most of the country anticipating the Allies' invasion of Western Europe, it was only natural that there would be continued questions and conversation about pro football players and their armed services status.

Lambeau addressed it in a talk to service clubs in Manitowoc and Two Rivers, saying there was an essential difference in the makeup needed for combat and that required in athletes. He said an athlete's physical weaknesses can be addressed by trainers, but the same weakness might lead to rejection by the army.

He said several members of his current Packers team had been turned down for military service while four from the 1943 team – Chet Adams, Dick Evans, Tony Canadeo and Andy Uram – had been drafted.

He anticipated that many of his recent draft choices would also be entering military service. In fact, he was right because none of the thirty-two draft picks in 1944 ever played a single game for the Packers. Not a one.

There was somber news in mid-May when the wife of former Packer Hal Van Every, a halfback on the 1940 and 1941 teams, said she was told by the War Department that he was missing in action. Van Every served on a bomber that was shot down. He became a prisoner of war and sent to Stalag Luft III, where he would not be liberated until April 1945. He would live until he was eighty-nine.

Former Packer Cecil Isbell, who last played for the team in 1942, was elevated to head football coach at Purdue University, his alma mater.

The Packers' 1944 schedule included three games at City Stadium in Green Bay, one more than in 1943 when the league operated with just eight teams. There would be two home games played at State Fair Park in Milwaukee.

The team also scheduled two practice games in early September – one at Baltimore against the Washington Redskins and one in Buffalo against the Boston Yanks. The team would spend four days at the U.S. Naval Training Center in Sampson, New York, prior to the Buffalo game.

***

Evidence of the war's reach was everywhere in the community, even at East High School, where the decorations for the annual school prom were minimized in order not to waste valuable paper products.

There were ongoing adjustments to tire rationing, with the periodic tire inspection requirements for passenger cars being eliminated. However, anyone seeking new tires or tubes had to undergo tire inspection first, and there remained a critical need for tires for commercial vehicles.

Most critical was the labor manpower shortage and a call went out for 125 women to take semiskilled positions. Needed were workers in retail and wholesale jobs, cheese processing plants, offices, packing companies, and furniture manufacturing. Before the school year ended, a plea went to the high schools to find students to work in food production during the summer.

Vacationing teachers no longer needed to get a statement of availability to accept summer employment under the War Manpower Commission's new plan. The war industries were depending upon the entrance of teachers into the seasonal workforce.

Local News Highlights

May 1: The Wisconsin Interscholastic Athletic Association warned high school boxing coaches that boxing is on trial in the state and that "crowd appeal" must be eliminated and "boy benefit" made the sole objective.

May 3: Green Bay Community Chest will get half of the proceeds from the sale of the waste paper collected by the Boy Scouts. The other half goes to the Boy Scouts organization.

May 8: The H.C. Prange Co., with a Mother's Day ad that says "She's a Hero Too" promoted its special mothers hat for $5 and $10 in its millinery section. Meanwhile, Stieffel's promoted special men's suits for $55 showing a man sitting comfortably in it while holding a cigarette.

May 17: Of the 657 Brown County men discharged so far from the service in World War II, 370 have filed claims for disability incurred or aggravated in the service.

May 22: Mayor Alex Biemeret declared the day Poppy Day in the city and called upon citizens to wear memorial poppies in honor of the men who have given their lives in the nation's defense.

May 26: Former Green Bay Bluejays outfielder Andy Pafko, now a rookie with the Chicago Cubs, was described by Cardinals manager Bill Southworth as the best young player in the league.

Leathem Smith Shipbuilding in Sturgeon Bay was awarded a contract to build four more 4,000-ton auxiliary freighters. It already had a contract to build sixteen of the new type of cargo ships, each at a cost of approximately $1,600,000.

But a Green Bay man who was sentenced to twenty years in prison for statutory rape was returned to the Waupun State Prison when he failed to show up for work regularly at the Sturgeon Bay shipyard, where he had been paroled to help with the wartime manpower shortage.

The actions of youth during wartime were topics of debate. The chairman of the national Counsel on Youth Delinquency came to Green Bay and sounded an alarm.

"A victorious conclusion of the war will be a hollow victory indeed for America unless the youth problem is solved first," said Dr. Morris G. Caldwell. "A rising tide of juvenile delinquency indicates that the home and community have failed."

News about health, careers, divorce and politics appeared before *Press-Gazette* readers.

Approximately 200 workers were getting x-rays daily to check for signs of tuberculosis. The tests were being made on a touring bus commissioned by the state board of health in an effort to detect early signs of the disease before it infected others.

Emblems signifying forty and fifty years of service as locomotive engineers were pinned on eight members of the Brotherhood of Locomotive Engineers at the Beaumont Hotel.

Brown County Judge Henry Graass granted a dozen divorces over a two-week period, so he had a sign posted in front of his bench. It showed a tousle-haired youngster kneeling beside his bed saying,

This photo from the Packers' 1943 training camp shows (from left) linemen Bill Kuusisto, Pete Gudauskas, Sherwood Fries, and Glen Sorenson. Kuusisto and Sorenson remained on the team for the 1944 championship season. (Green Bay Press-Gazette photo)

"Dear God. Please make Mama and Papa stop fighting. It's hard to take sides."

A clothing campaign for Russian relief was started, and plans were underway to obtain a suitable vacant store in downtown Green Bay to store the clothes.

State Senator John W. Byrnes announced that he was a candidate for the Eighth Congressional District seat. He would run as a Republican.

The Brown County Board took a major step into its future when it adopted the resolution from the special airport committee to exercise options on sufficient land in the town of Ashwaubenon for a Class 4 airport. The land would eventually become part of the Austin Straubel Airport.

**

Readers of the *Green Bay Press-Gazette* were fed a daily series of letters to the People's Forum that reflected some of the mindset of the community. The paper set some guidelines:

"The Press-Gazette cannot print anonymous communications. The rule is not an idle one. Unless people have enough interest in their disclosures to advise this newspaper of their identity, although that identity will not be divulged, the paper cannot give them space.

"The *Press-Gazette* will not publish any further Forum poems after today so long as newsprint restrictions continue, except those sent in by members of the armed forces."

Letters came in.

May 1 - I could send you more details of what is going on in Italy but censorship rulings make it practically impossible to do so. The best way to get an idea of the life over here is to read Ernie Pyle's columns when he is writing about the infantry, anyway, and that is most of the time.

Ernie is a great favorite because he's the only writer who gives the folks at home any idea of the dirty, wearying, grinding, half-normal life we live and he doesn't make any bones about saying that the infantry lives like that.

- Soldier

May 9 - There has been a lot of rather mean propaganda circulating around the country trying to create the impression that our citizen population were laying down on their job and were altogether too complacent about the war situation. This, of course, is old stuff started some time ago down there in Washington by the brass hats and chair warming barnacles.

Forgotten Man
Green Bay

May 10 - Many articles have lately appeared in the press referring to the peace terms submitted by Russia to Finland. The writers in many cases offer their advice to the Finns to get out of the war, but do not volunteer any suggestions how this can be accomplished except by blindly accepting Russia's demands.

Very True Yours
V. Berg

May 11 - There are going to be many kinds of economic problems for agriculture after this war, but one of the biggest, in my opinion, can be stated rather simply. The finding of a good market for all the American farmer wants to produce and can produce within the limits of sound farming methods.

Henry McAbee, a farmer
West De Pere

Quarterbacks were not the only position players who threw the ball during this era, at least in publicity photos. Pictured (from left) are back Paul Duhart, end Ray Wehba, tailback Irv Comp, and halfback Lou Brock. (Green Bay Press-Gazette photo)

May 12 - In the paper for the last few months have been articles concerning the coming election. These letters are written by the same old Republican town criers, who are always belly-aching and crying about the war going too slow, Roosevelt being a dictator, seizure of Montgomery Ward and dozens of other things. So win the war and peace faster with Franklin D. Roosevelt's fourth term.

The Observing Kid

Green Bay

May 17 - I am glad to see that some interest is being shown in suitable club-rooms for the Disabled American Veterans. Surely, of all the people returning from our wars, these men are the most deserving and needful.

W. Earl Fogleson
De Pere

May 23 - When man has to fight for his Constitutional right, or even just for his place in the sunshine, and has to use deceit, malicious lies and cheating of every sort - and the whole process is called propaganda - well, things have come to a pretty pass. It is comforting to know that the Republicans are taking a stand against it. But we have to do more than take a stand – we must all fight it with all our might.

Betsy Ross
Green Bay

May 25 - If Roosevelt is re-elected for a fourth term, he has then got a mandate and Americanism will die as did the Roman empire and those that have gone before.

The Observing Old Timer

May 27 - Time has taught us that, had the world determined to accept and diligently completed and prosecuted President Woodrow Wilson's idea of a League of Nations, it would have averted our second world war.

John W. Arney
Green Bay

May 31 - I happen to want news as fast as it happens. I don't want Army censors holding up news. I want the news today, not tomorrow or two months from now. I'm quite sure that the boys way out there on Attu and Honolulu feel the same way.

E.W.J., Green Bay

***

Editor V.I. (Victor) Minahan had the final word on editorials.

The Blacks and the Whites in America
May 5, 1944

In the figures concerning the rejection of young men from the army recently published by the American Medical Journal may be found a powerful sermon against the prevailing treatment of the Negro in America and what it means in health to the individual and ability to the nation.

Of every 1000 whites examined 237 were rejected. Of every 1000 Negroes examined 455 were rejected. When the South complains, as it often does, that its economic condition is not on a par with the North, does it ever consider how far it is responsible for this unhappy state because of the economic conditions in which it holds the black man?

But No Fighting, Please
May 9, 1944

We have over 50,000 Italians in this country who were captured in North Africa. They are young, healthy, hardened and battle-experienced. Their lawful government has joined hands with us to crush Germany. Legally and morally, therefore, these men are available to us for the heavy and bitter work of fighting. But we would not think of thus employing them.

Schoolboys and Conservation
May 15, 1944

The Wisconsin Conservation Commission acted wisely when it renewed an arrangement with Boy Scouts for a forestry camp in the Northern Highland State Forest and ceded buildings and land at an abandoned CCC camp to the Boy Scouts organization for use in summer recreation activities.

Office workers at Fort Howard Paper Company in Green Bay in 1943. (Photo courtesy of University of Wisconsin-Green Bay Archives)

B'nai B'rith Produces Some Facts
May 22, 1944

A fellowship organization of the Jewish religion has sent out to the press a record of some of larger aspects of accomplishments in the war by those of the Jewish faith. The organization feels that the whispered slur that those of Jewish faith are dodging their responsibilities should be met with proof, with pictures, names, post office addresses, and even casualty lists to show how vicious as well as how false are the deadly whispers.

Green Bay and Its War Wrecks
May 25, 1944

Articles have been printed in the Press-Gazette at irregular times in order to keep the public informed of our great human stake in this war, the thousands of men from hereabouts that we have sent forth to battle and the trickle that is now growing into a rivulet as our maimed and mutilated return with dulled eye and enervated body. Let us try at least to make a stab at keeping some of our promises. Before this conflict is ended this community will have upon its hands crippled young bodies to a number that none of us cares to think about but all of us must.

Memorial Day
May 30, 1944

On the eve of this Memorial Day is the official statement of the War Department that our casualties have far passed 200,000 and that our actual dead, the admitted as well as the probables among the missing, is fast climbing to 100,000.

It is in this hour, charged with the cannons' hoarse roar, that the future takes on such tremendous possibilities because of the willing sacrifice of our splendid youths to what is conceived to be the safety, the security and the future of the nation.

The participants, and whether living or dead, have established records making it imperative for us to give our best of heart and mind to be merely worthy of them.

***

(The following war updates were provided by Major John M. Walter in his role as the orientation and communications officer at Camp Wolters in Mineral Wells, Texas. He wrote the daily war updates for the base and included them in his personal diary.)

May 1, 1944 - All the day's news centers around Allied assaults on Axis ground objectives ... 3,000 bombers pound at German anti-invasion targets ... it was the 17th day of history's greatest sustained air offensive ... Soviet planes blast at Idritsa in Latvia, and the U.S.S.R. shows signs of chafing anew over the delay in establishing a western land front ... Italian harbors of Genoa, La Spezia and Livorno are pasted ... In Southwest Pacific, fliers move activities northwest of captured Hollandia with attacks on Schouten and Wadke islands on the route to the Philippines ... Sorong in Dutch New Guinea also hit ...

Nazi convoy off Norwegian coast attacked successfully by British carrier-based planes.

May 4, 1944 - Great air offensive against Germany goes into 20th day, with special attention paid to French communications system ... Soviet planes make widespread attacks in Rumania and old Poland ... Nazi supply lines in northern Italy pounded by bombers ... Mistaken identity causes fight between U.S. air and naval forces in the Pacific; we lose two PT boats and two planes ... Japs bearing down on Hsuchang in Honan province of China, and are building up for a new offensive against Imphal in India.

May 11, 1944 - Europe plastered with 4,500 tons of bombs in past 24 hours ... it was 26th consecutive day of uninterrupted aerial offensive ... Complete collapse of Jap defenses in North Hollandia, New Guinea ... 621 Allied prisoners, including 462 Sikhs, were recaptured, in addition to 259 Jap prisoners ... The crack Japanese 18th Army, which took Singapore, is trapped by Stilwell's army in northern Burma ... Chinese face crisis in Honan province, with Loyang cut off on three sides ... Japs have crossed Yellow river northwest of city ... For the second day, German troops on the Italian Adriatic flank have withdrawn before British.

May 16, 1944 - Lower half of Gustav line in central Italy is shredded by French and American troops, while British appear close to a breakthrough near Cassino ... U.S. troops have taken Sant Maria Infante and are pressing on toward Spigno ... Soviet airmen batter Wow, hit Nazi convoy in N Norwegian port of Kirkenes ... other American aircraft hit Tru and Ponape in Carolines ... also plastered are Wadke and Schouten islands off Dutch New Guinea coast ... In Burma, Stilwell's forces have captured Tarongyang, and are only 10 miles north of Kamaing ... 150 miles to the east Chinese forces have crossed Salween river and are moving westward in effort to link Burma and Ledo roads.

May 22, 1944 - Americans capture Fondi as Allied drive northward in Italy continues ... they are 30 airline miles from the Anzio beachhead ... action flares up on the beachhead as U.S. patrol penetrates 500 yards into German positions ... Aleutian-based Liberators raid Ketoi and Shimushiri islands, within 400 miles of Jap mainland, and Flying Dragons from China bomb Pratas island, 275 miles from Philippines ... Soviets repulse German attack on lower Dniester ... 3,000 Allied planes, mostly fighters, strafe German-held Europe, hitting every moving military object behind Atlantic wall.

May 27, 1944 - Allies are pushing Germans from a defense line 16 miles south of Rome ... battle centers at Velletri ... Americans drive past Cisterna to capture mountain strong point of Cori ... Japs cling to part of Myitkyina in Burma ... Chungking announced that cutting of Burma Road by Chinese was in error. They captured Chifang, not Chefang ... Loyang has fallen to Japs in Honan ... Rail yards at Lyon in France are bombed ... during past week 32,000 Allied planes battered pre-invasion targets with 35,000 tons of bombs ... Biak island in Philippines pasted by Liberators.

May 31, 1944 - Americans and British gain slowly 16 miles from Rome in the Alban hills ... Ardea, three miles from the coast, falls to the Allies ... 1,000 planes from Italy hit aircraft factories in Austria, Yugoslavia ... Americans defeat Japs in first Pacific tank battle on Biak island, but defenders of Biak airports are extremely stubborn ... Germans attacking Soviets north of Iasi in Rumania.

June 1944

Throbbing Spectacle

The elephant in every American community's room when the month began was the promise of an invasion in western Europe to provide the two-front vise against the Nazis and hopefully hasten the conclusion of that part of the world war.

On Monday, June 5, *Green Bay Press-Gazette* readers learned that their countrymen were sweeping through Rome and ridding that Italian capital of Germans.

The war also impacted news closer to home. The Green Bay Office of Defense Transportation said it was reducing the amount of gas for school busses in the nearby Pulaski, Coleman and Oconto Falls school districts because they used the busses to transport students to a music festival in Oconto, a violation of the ODT's orders. The busses were only supposed to carry students to and from school.

Secretary of State Fred Zimmerman sought an opinion from Wisconsin attorney general John Martin whether Marine Capt. Joseph McCarthy, on leave as a circuit judge, could have his name on the ballot as a Republican candidate for US Senate.

The Kewaunee Shipbuilding and Engineering Corporation proudly christened the sixty-ninth vessel it had produced during the war.

The Green Bay Elks Club ran a full-page ad in the *Press-Gazette* to announce its sponsorship of an effort to recruit men from age seventeen to fifty to be trained as radio technicians for the US Navy.

Eighty-three students were preparing for graduation ceremonies at De Pere High School the next day, with more than a quarter of them already committed either to joining a branch of the armed services, or contributing to the war effort by working on farms or at war-related industries.

And the community's fifth war loan campaign was launched with Don Fairbairn as chairman and a goal to raise $5,989,000.

But non-war related events continued to proceed.

On that Monday, the Packers opened their ticket office to begin selling tickets for the three 1944 games at City Stadium in Green Bay and the two games at State Fair Park in Milwaukee.

Mary Vogels prepares tickets for distribution, sorted by stadium section, in the Packers' ticket office, August 2, 1946. (Green Bay Press-Gazette photo)

Local News Highlights

June 3: The eight bridge tenders petitioned the Green Bay city council for an eight-hour day to replace the current 12-hour shifts.

June 7: More than 400 school patrol youth were treated to huge servings of booyah at Bay Beach to signal the end of the school year.

June 10: Householders in the Green Bay area were warned to fill their coal bins during the summer months to be certain of having an adequate supply next winter. The shortage of motor trucks and drivers for coal distribution was critical.

June 16: The Office of Price Administration sought an injunction against a Sturgeon Bay preserving company, alleging it didn't meet the price ceiling restrictions in the sale of red cherries.

June 22: Cal Hubbard, the former Packer great and current American League umpire, said this baseball season has been the toughest ever because there are so many more close plays.

St. Willebrord's Catholic Church announced that thirty-one eighth graders had graduated from its school in downtown Green Bay.

And relief was felt when the two Milson brothers, Bert, age thirteen, and Stuart, age ten, were found safe after being adrift on the bay for fourteen hours before being rescued. Both boys would go on to successful medical careers in Green Bay.

Entertainment on that Monday for those who chose the cinema was the latest popular movie *Lost Angels,* starring young Margaret O'Brien at the Orpheum, and *The Song of Bernadette,* starring Jennifer Jones, at the De Pere Theater.

When most of the community awoke on Tuesday, June 6, it began to absorb the news of an event called D-Day, the massive invasion on the shores of Normandy in northern France. The *Press-Gazette,* which went to press in the afternoon, blared the headline "D-Day Off to Good Start" across the top of the front page.

The editorial page took note in the days that followed.

This Is It
June 7, 1944

The throbbing spectacle along the coast of Normandy yesterday was without parallel. It held the world agog with breathless wonder.

Our faith in the ultimate conclusion has never lagged despite the heartbreaking price we expect must be paid. But the amount of that price and the period over which it must be expended will depend on the morale of the enemy troops since we have no doubt that the defenses have been constructed with an efficiency for which Teuton tribes have long been noted.

Spectacular and awe-inspiring is the present phase of the battle. The far more important thing for us concerns itself with our interests and unknown ability to keep the battle moving steadily and inexorably to the East.

The President's Warning
June 8, 1944

Perhaps other parts of the President's recent statement were given far more attention, and listed as much more interesting, than his warning not to let our optimism over the successful early stages of the invasion run away with us, but the admonition he spoke was both worthy and seasonable.

Any expectation that we are going to march through France the way the Germans did four years ago is built on pretty bubbles.

Something Is the Matter
June 9, 1944

While perhaps 15,000 of our men were dying on foreign battlefields, on Wednesday last another 15,000 pettishly and contemptuously left their work benches at the Wright Aeronautics plant at Lockland, Ohio, because, in the rush of war work, seven Negro workers had been transferred to a department manned heretofore by whites.

There is something poisonous in the blood stream of a nation that can tolerate conduct of this kind as a patient parent puts up with the antics of a four-year-old distrained child, and the fault is not alone that of those who so grossly misbehaved. In such contingency he is merely another yellow deserter.

Peace Now Or Else
June 10, 1944

If we can save the precious figure of Peace out of this conflict and embalm it like one of the Pharaohs, and if we can also provide a workable system to relieve the billion people who are now vassals of the empires from oppression that smothers them, then the continuing brutality of the war, whether for five or fifteen years more, is not an unreasonable price to pay for that result.

Our Casualties in France
June 14, 1944

Although American losses are painful, they are far below what the command expected. In one form or another the above statement has been used constantly since the landings in France. It seems next to meaningless. Why are we not told our losses?

As the Battle Goes
June 15, 1944

No one in America should become lightheaded about our apparent successes. But since Pearl Harbor we have a record that entitles us to indulge in a reasonable amount of enlivened satisfaction if not exultation. Whom the gods destroy they first make swell-headed.

American Casualties and a Toehold in France
June 20, 1944

Late last Saturday, our army in France announced that the invasion and subsequent battle covering eleven days had cost us less than 16,000 casualties, which included about 25 percent slain.

If British and Canadian forces equaled our own in France, and if their casualties were no more, the invasion to date has not been as expensive in bloodshed as we expected. Five to ten times these casualties were anticipated in many informal quarters.

But we should, on the other hand, appraise more accurately our accomplishments in France. For we have not accomplished a real toehold.

If the Germans Could See
June 21, 1944

Any sort of ruse would be golden if it could induce the German army to approach the ocean and watch an invasion by the Allied forces. They would see an armada more vast and more potent than any that was ever floated. They would realize that all the warships constructed by the Reich and which they were led to believe would be formidable adversaries of ours could not live within sight of our naval forces more than minutes.

President Advises Caution
June 26, 1944

Wisely did Mr. Roosevelt advise the country that the going of our armies in France will be slow, painful and uncertain for many weary months to come. He set forth the problem in figures by saying that we did not yet possess one-tenth of one percent of French soil. All that may now be said is that we have made a good beginning.

Our Success and Our Future Troubles
June 27, 1944

Victory has perched upon the staff that carries our fluttering flag everywhere. Already we rule the air everywhere we can find landing fields. Already we rule the waves everywhere we go.

But we must not forget something our enemies forgot. For while victory was riding high with them, they neglected to observe that in their prepared condition victory was to be had for almost the taking. We must not be similarly misled into a deceptive feeling of satisfaction.

***

The initial response from the civilian population was to pray as news of the invasion arrived over radio. An estimated 8,000 people assembled in their respective Green Bay churches that Tuesday night to pray for success of the invasion and support of the allied troops.

Green Bay mayor Alex Biemeret issued a proclamation urging citizens to participate in church services and Bishop Paul P. Rhode asked members of the area's Catholic churches to attend special services that evening. The general response was so large that several churches were filled to capacity and needed to set up chairs in the aisles.

St. Mary's Catholic Church in De Pere decided to conduct novena services for nine straight days and the Knights of Columbus planned a special invasion prayer hour at St. Francis Cathedral. The K.C. Bridge Club planned to attend that service and hold its usual games afterwards.

The community would learn later that Staff Sgt. Eugene Farley of Green Bay had a surprise waiting for him when he boarded a landing ship on D-Day. The jeep parked next to him was covered with Green Bay Packers signs. Turns out it was the work of fellow Green Bay man, Staff Sgt. Alfred Maes.

The war's impact was everywhere. Selective Service announced that farm workers classified 2-C could take canning factory jobs in the Green Bay area as long as farm production wasn't impaired.

Three German prisoners of war were being sought after they escaped from Camp Au Train near Marquette, Michigan. They had been assigned to the lumber industry.

Word was sent out that employment ceilings would be established for Green Bay plants as more stringent manpower regulations go into effect.

The invasion was cited as a contributing factor in the community's drive to meet its war bond quota, with the volunteers showing more enthusiasm.

The Green Bay post office established a special uniform airmail letter card that could be sent to American prisoners of war. The only cards available were those that could be sent to prisoners in Europe.

But not everything was positive. W.D. Baker, executive secretary of general salvage for the state's War Production Board, told community leaders that the paper shortage was far more critical than scrap metal and rubber had ever been, and the state was only producing half of the waste paper it should. He said paper was now as vital as airplanes, tanks and other equipment.

With the schools closing for the summer, eighty Green Bay boys and twenty-five from De Pere were set to begin railroad maintenance work near Forest Junction south of Green Bay under the supervision of high school football coaches Frosty Ferzacca and Dad Braisher.

And the graduating seniors at West High School gave the school a gift of three war savings bonds, having a maturity value of $300, to be spent on a postwar sound system for the school auditorium.

Also on the education front, the director of the state elementary school association told a Green Bay audience that too many teachers in the state public schools weren't qualified, but were needed because of the manpower shortage. He noted that 1,228 teachers graduated from state teacher colleges in 1943, but only 463 graduated in 1944.

Taverns made the news.

A petition from the Brown County Ministerial Association and eleven west side clergymen asked that a license be refused for a tavern at the intersection of West Mason and Taylor streets on the far west end of Green Bay. They cited an 1895 ordinance restricting the issuance of tavern licenses for establishments west of Broadway, which parallels the Fox River in the middle of the city. The ordinance had never been repealed or amended.

And the Wisconsin Supreme Court upheld as constitutional the tavern closing law that prohibited the sale of beer and liquor between 1 and 8 a.m. in all establishments outside Milwaukee County.

Brown County sheriff Andrew Los said the number of slot machines in the county were "down" and would remain down in the future.

There was news that had a future impact. More than 450 acres of

Three years after 450 acres of land had been set aside for a new Green Bay airport, workers finally began clearing operations on June 3, 1947. The facility today is known as Austin Straubel International Airport, named for Maj. Austin Straubel, who was Brown County's first aviation loss in World War II. Straubel played football at Green Bay East under coach Curly Lambeau, and later at the University of Wisconsin. (Green Bay Press-Gazette photo)

land in Ashwaubenon and Hobart was being set aside for the new Green Bay airport. And the Green Bay YMCA acquired thirty-two acres of land on the east shore of Green Bay near the village of Fairland in Door County. It would be used as a recreation center and family camp.

Nobody knew it at the time because the dots hadn't connected yet, but a unique coincidence centered around Green Bay native Jim Crowley. The former East High football player, who went on to star in Knute Rockne's famed Four Horseman backfield at the University of Notre Dame, reached the rank of lieutenant commander in the US Navy and served first in the South Pacific and then as athletic director at the Sampson, New York, Naval Training Station.

In early June, he signed a contract to be head coach of the pro football Boston Yankees once the war ended, a role he never fulfilled because he instead became the first commissioner of the new All-American Football League in 1946.

The dots? Crowley was coached at East High by Earl "Curly" Lambeau in 1919, the same year Lambeau formed the Packers. When Crowley became head coach at Fordham University in the 1930s, he led a team that gained fame on the backs of an offensive line known as the "Seven Blocks of Granite." One of those linemen was future Packers coach Vince Lombardi. No one would ever match that Lambeau-Lombardi connection.

***

There was Packers football news during this historic month. Lambeau, seeking to fill an assistant coaching spot vacated by the departure of Richard (Red) Smith, announced mid-month that he hired

Don Hutson (left) takes in practice along with Curly Lambeau (center) and line coach George Trafton. Trafton was a star center for the Chicago Staleys before they became the Bears, and thus hated by most Packers fans. (Green Bay Press-Gazette photo)

longtime Chicago Bears lineman George (Brute) Trafton to coach Packers linemen.

Trafton was a character who at the time was running a boxing gymnasium in Chicago and also serving as manager and owner of pro boxers. He was a high school classmate in 1919 of Hunk Anderson, another Notre Dame standout. Anderson was one of three Fighting Irish players who were kicked off the team after they were caught playing for the Packers under assumed names in 1921.

Trafton was a highly skilled professional lineman and would be inducted into the Pro Football Hall of Fame's second class in 1964. But for 1944, he would team up with Hutson as assistants to Lambeau.

Longtime Packers fans might have been surprised by the hiring of Trafton, since one journalist wrote that he was "strongly disliked in every NFL city except Green Bay and Rock Island, where he was hated."

Edward Prell, writing for the *Chicago Tribune:* "If it weren't for Lt. Comdr. George Halas being thousands of miles away, maybe George Trafton would not have done what he did. He has gone over to the enemy. When he was at the height of his career, he was a public enemy up in the north country."

Trafton was Halas's starting center for the Chicago Staleys in 1921, before they became the Bears.

This was the month that Lambeau started signing players for the 1944 season.

The first contract to come in was from former Texas running back Roy D. McKay. He had been drafted by the Packers in 1943, but went into the army. He received his honorable discharge and was ready to play pro football. Since he had been unable to play in the College All-Star game in 1943 because of his military commitment, he would play in the 1944 game, then report to the Packers.

Next came the signed contract of Elijah Pope (Pete) Tinsley, a veteran guard also with an honorable discharge from the army. He had to leave the service because of chronic arthritis and ear problems. Tinsley was working for a house painting and washing business in

Coach Curly Lambeau supervises a blocking drill. The fact the player is in full game uniform indicates this was set up for the photo op. (Green Bay Press-Gazette photo)

Green Bay, and said the previous year that he was finished with football. But he wasn't.

Then came four more contracts: running back Don Perkins, tackle Norbert Evers, halfback Bob McRoberts, and guard Ervin Dzierewski. Of the bunch, only Perkins would make it to the 1944 Packers roster.

One player guaranteed to make it, and who signed his contract in late June, was center Charley Brock. He was working a night shift for an industrial company producing wartime products and had already established himself as one of the premiere centers in pro football.

***

(The following war updates were provided by Major John M. Walter in his role as the orientation and communications officer at Camp Wolters in Mineral Wells, Texas. He wrote the daily war updates for the base and included them in his personal diary.)

June 3, 1944 - Bomber bases for United States planes have been opened in the Soviet Union, promising shuttle action against Germany ... Nazis gain again at Iasi in Rumania ... Ridge overlooking Biak island airfield in Pacific has been taken by Americans, and Jap snipers wiped out ... 7,000 more tons of explosives drop on Hitler's Europe ... German paratroops capture Marshal Tito's headquarters in Yugoslavia, but Broz himself escapes ... Velletri and Valmontone fall to Allies in advance on Rome, and the 5th Army nears the capital's outskirts ... Berlin claims Rome will not be defended.

June 6, 1944 - Today was D-Day for Europe ... before dawn, following a terrific aerial bombardment of the French coast, thousands of airborne and seaborne Allied troops poured onto the Norman peninsula, somewhere between Cherbourg and La Havre ... initial reports indicated that casualties were light, and control soon was extended over most of the peninsula ... General Dwight Eisenhower is in command ... 4,000 first line ships operated in the English channel, and 11,000 planes provided air cover ... the channel islands of Guernsey and Jersey were mopped up ... In Italy, Allied forces have driven 10 miles past Rome, and Lt. Gen. Clark's 5th Army is pushing toward the Campagna, suitable for tank action ... Six Japanese columns are closing in on Changsha in Hunan province of China, with one column only 25 miles from the city ... 60 miles north, the Japs crossed Lake Tung Ting for the third time in a week ... American and Chinese forces inched ahead another 400 yards in Myitkyina, Burma.

Awakened at 0610 by a telephone call from Lt. Walrath, telling me of the invasion, and soon was on the way to camp. It turned into a very busy day.

Took my portable radio to camp and had it turned on most of the day. At 1300 gave 17th Hour Orientation lecture to 60th Battalion. Everyone was preoccupied with invasion news and it didn't go off too well, I felt. Back at branch, listened to radio news and wrote supplemental war bulletin to keep troops posted on developments during the day.

Sat around listening to radio, which was full of invasion reports and highly patriotic. Bob Hope, comedian, put aside the funny stuff at a California air field, and gave a fine talk. President Roosevelt led the nation in prayer. It was a sober evening, with many a soldier on continental duty wishing he were overseas.

June 7, 1944 - D-Day plus one ... Allies expand invasion front along 50 miles of French coast ... Berlin announces new landings in Calais area ... steady streams of reinforcements are pouring across the channel to the Normandy peninsula ... weather has been bad, with high seas and strong wind ... the Luftwaffe still has not appeared in strength ... German coastal batteries still are being shelled by naval vessels ... 'The Allied armies will meet in Berlin, predicted Red Star as the Soviets dusted off another offensive ... all Soviet papers carried huge photos of Gen. Eisenhower ... Chinese-American stranglehold tightened around Myitkyina in Burma ... Japs have reached outskirts of Changsha in Hunan province, but fall back in Honan ... In Italy, Allied 5th Army swarms across Tiber river, pursues retreating Germans against weak resistance ... French troops capture Vitoli northeast of Rome.

June 10, 1944 - Americans have cut communication lines to Cherbourg on Normandy peninsula ... the town of Ste. Mere Eglise has been taken and General Eisenhower reports satisfactory progress along the entire front ... the sector is about the size of the late Anzio beachhead ... fighting is severe around Caen ... Nazis lose two destroyers in brush with British in channel ... 5th Army continues to chase Germans up the Italian peninsula, and now is 55 miles above Rome ... The Germans are beginning to withdraw along the Adriatic coast ... Nazis repulsed by Soviets near Tarnopol in old Poland ... General Marshall, General Arnold and Admiral King are in London ...Allied planes sink four Jap destroyers trying to reinforce Biak positions ... Japs are seven and a half miles from Changsha in Hunan province, but are taking a beating along the Salween river in Yunnan, and are about surrounded at Myitkyina in Burma.

Boy Scouts enjoy their freshly pitched tents during the Camporee at State Fair Park in Milwaukee, June 17, 1944. (Green Bay Press-Gazette photo)

June 17, 1944 - American troops are three-fourths of the way across the Cherbourg peninsula ... strategic St. Saveur has been captured ... Montebourg has been regained ... French forces invade island of Elba from north and south ... U.S. gives passports to Finnish Minister Procope ... RAF shifts air war, bombs Berlin, Duisburg ... fighters smash at robot coast base in France ... U.S. task force bags 47 Jap planes in Bonins raid ... troops edge ahead at Saipan against heavy mortar fire.

June 20, 1944 - In greatest Pacific battle since Midway, 300 Jap aircraft are destroyed in attack on U.S. carrier force off Saipan ... Aslito airdrome on that island has been captured ... Conquest of Elba is completed by French, with capture of 1,800 Nazi prisoners ... on mainland 8th Army captured Perugia, communications center between Rome and Florence ... Soviet troops are less than 10 miles from Viipuri, and the poor Finns are the next thing to being knocked out of the war ... Germans are thrown back to main defense line six miles below Cherbourg in Normandy.

June 28, 1944 - Thomas Dewey and John Bricker nominated by Republicans at Chicago to run for president and vice-president against Franklin Roosevelt ... British driving ahead along 6 and half mile front in Caen area of Normandy ... 20,000 Germans were captured when Cherbourg fell ... 3,082 U.S. troops have been killed in French invasion ... Soviets drive toward Minsk in White Russia, capturing Mogilev ... 5th Army is 32 miles below Livorno in Italy, while inland British reach Castiglione del Lago ... Jap garrison at Mogaung wiped out as that Burma base falls to Allies ... Japs are flanking Hengyang in Hunan province.

July 1944

Pollution at Bay Beach

Sunny and warm weather greeted northeastern Wisconsin on the Independence holiday weekend, but there were challenges facing those on the home front.

The War Production Board's salvage division said Green Bay and Brown County were falling far short of their desired quotas with waste paper collection, and it scheduled a Waste Paper Week for the second week of July. Homeowners were urged to reuse paper bags and bring bags with them when they shopped for groceries.

The Office of Price Administration (OPA) said it might have to establish rent controls on Green Bay landlords because some were continuing to raise rents. An extensive survey showed that unnecessary evictions were occurring. This was critical because it was making it difficult for the area's war industries to recruit the necessary manpower to operate at capacity.

And the state OPA found 128 violations of gasoline rationing regulations among the 388 motorists checked in fifteen Wisconsin cities on the eve of the July Fourth holiday.

A full-page ad in the July 14 *Green Bay Press-Gazette* bemoaned the fact that the sale of war bonds to individuals was not going well.

"Brown County is not proud of its record on the sale of bonds to individuals so far. Here's how we stand: $3,488,000 (individual quota for county) $1,955,237 (sales to individuals thru July 13) $1,532,763 (balance to go by July 31)."

At the same time, waste paper collection was the largest in one day, but still yielded only about half of the six pounds per capita set as the goal for the city of Green Bay and the towns of Allouez and Preble.

***

War news dominated and brought reports of military gains while never skipping over the reality of conflict.

Once a week, the *Press-Gazette* published the report from the War Department that listed the number of Americans either missing or assumed to be prisoners of war. On Monday, July 17, it announced the names of 1,008 soldiers missing in action, with 522 assumed to be prisoners of war. The *Press-Gazette* printed the names of every Wisconsin soldier on that list, including the city they were from and the name of their closest relative.

Boy Scouts Howard Schmidt, LeRoy Brunette and Dick Cornell pick up waste paper on July 10, 1944. (Green Bay Press-Gazette photo)

Local News Highlights

July 8: A disabled German tank captured during the North African campaign drew large crowds when it was put on display on North Jefferson Street.

July 11: More than 100 boys, girls and elders from the Green Bay area traveled to Door County to help harvest the bumper crop of cherries. Many were Boy Scouts and several families were included.

July 13: Casey Stengel, recently named manager of the Milwaukee Brewers minor league baseball team, was a guest at a Victory Industrial Baseball League game at Joannes Park.

July 22: Preliminary work starts on a new passenger depot for the Milwaukee Road at the Oakland Avenue site. The cost is estimated at $50,000.

July 26: The Green Bay engineering firm of Foth, Boyd and Porath was awarded the contract to draw a master plan for the new Brown County airport.

But there were bright spots to keep spirits buoyed. Boy Scouts on Washington Island shipped 14,000 pounds of waste paper to the U.S. Paper Mill in De Pere. The paper was transported free of charge on a small freighter, and the scouts were paid $98 for their work.

A clear sign of the times was the fact there was a record number of work permits issued to boys and girls under the age of eighteen from July 1943 to July 1, 1944. The previous one-year record was 1,872, while the recent year saw 3,040 permits issued.

A further sign of the times came mid-month when the Brown County Board of Park Commissioners voted to meet with the Metropolitan Sewerage District and the Harbor Commission to see if any measures could be taken to eliminate pollution from the waters at Bay Beach. Tests had shown the water was unsafe for swimming, and the cause was believed to be industrial pollution.

Brown County parks superintendent Marshall Simons said fisher-

Newspaper Ads Ranged From Vitamins to Planes

Newspaper advertising in the summer of 1944 gave Green Bay area businesses the format to dangle their wares before the public.

Optometrist G.A. Michael, whose office was in the Bellin Building, was selling a Zenith Radionics Hearing Aid, complete with crystal microphone and miniature radio tubes. It cost $40.

The Larsen Orchard was dispatching trucks to communities of Greenleaf, Morrison and De Pere to transport anyone twelve years old and older who will pick the ripe cherries. Half of the crop would go to the government.

Holzer's Corner Drug Store at Washington and Pine streets was offering 100 vitamin D capsules for $3.39.

The C. Reiss Coal Company was selling Pocohantas briquets, calling them the "new, improved modern fuel."

Brauel's Grocery on Webster Avenue offered lobster tails at 79 cents per pound.

Ford Hopkins Drugs on North Washington Street sold a Genuine Shave Brush with a flat stand-up base for 89 cents.

Bogda Service Center at Cedar and Jefferson streets had Purina Chows to sell for mink, rabbits, dogs, goats and foxes.

The Doll House Beauty Shoppe on Monroe Avenue was providing women customers with a new hairstyle called the Lamour for $3.95.

Cohen's Department Store, Main Street at Jefferson, had ladies shoes from $1.47 to $2.97 a pair in what was billed as Ration Free offer. The shoes were part of a surplus so buyers didn't have to use shoe ration stamps to buy them.

Wartime restrictions were lifted so the manager of the Brown County Airport was offering lessons for anyone who wanted to learn to fly. The ad read, "Plane sales are again permissible. Enjoy traveling in your own plane."

men may catch unlimited pickerel from the Bay Beach lagoons because the fish have been killing area ducks.

Green Bay policemen began taking a course in judo to learn the science of disabling or even killing an armed opponent with one's bare hands, said Inspector H.J. Bero.

Wisconsin Public Service loaned eight fourteen-quart pressure cookers to the Vocational School kitchen to be used by area housewives for canning. The cost would be five cents per cooker.

Railroad officials were puzzled by the unexpected light passenger business after the July Fourth holiday weekend. The North Western and Milwaukee Road put on extra coaches in anticipation of heavy south-bound travelers, but the coaches were only partly filled.

And a representative of the National Foundation for Infantile Paralysis (polio) was in Green Bay to meet with leaders about the campaign for a projected county survey to aid in combatting the disease.

***

Editorial page opinions in the *Press-Gazette* took on such topics as Hitler, housewives and Democrats.

Sparing Hitler
July 12, 1944

H.G. Wells, the well-known British author, has started a small dust whirlwind by warning against executing Herr Hitler lest a martyr be made out of "a poor, crazy Austrian imbecile." Most people, however, bank upon Hitler solving the problem by removing himself from this tempestuous world. It will be one suicide devoutly to be hoped for.

Women as Candidates
July 14, 1944

Chilton produces the only woman this year who is intrepid enough to become a candidate for a major state office. Women as candidates are still scarce enough to be novelties.

Presumably, many men who would normally be available for legislative nominations are today occupied elsewhere, notably in the business of war.

The Fighting Housewife
July 22, 1944

To the earnest and diligent women of America who have helped in the war effort far beyond their modest admissions, we have no hesitation in asking further regard to one of the needs of a fighting country although it has and will appear in each instance small if not trivial. Grease and waste paper are as important as shells and food.

The Boss Who Never Quite Keeps His Word
July 25, 1944

The Democratic convention realized the importance of a wise selection for vice-president because of the swift aging of Mr. Roosevelt and the serious doubt concerning the present condition of his health. The nomination of Senator Truman was an improvement over Mr. Wallace by such large proportions.

***

July was a time to sign up more players for the 1944 season for Lambeau and the Packers. Some who signed contracts would make it on the team's roster by the start of the season. Some wouldn't make the cut.

The first to sign was Len Calgary, a Hurley (Wisconsin) native who played fullback and center for the University of Wisconsin, but quit football in 1943 to concentrate on his studies in the UW's

Irv Comp
(Press-Gazette photo)

There were no cheesehead hats to be seen during the 1940s as fans dressed in their Sunday best for games. This City Stadium crowd watched the Green Bay Packers beat the Cleveland Rams 45-28 on October 18, 1942. (Green Bay Press-Gazette photo)

College of Agriculture.

A few days later, Irv Comp signed for his second season, having been the Packers' second draft pick a year earlier. The Milwaukee native, who played collegiately at St. Benedict in Kansas, proved himself an accomplished passer, bettered only in his rookie season by Washington's Sammie Baugh and the Bears' Sid Luckman.

Then Lambeau got a signed contract from guard Charlie Tollefson, the one-time member of the "Iron Men" at the University of Iowa in 1939. He blocked for Heisman Trophy winner Nile Kinnick. Tollefson played some football on teams organized in the army and was honorably discharged.

Glen Sorenson, a guard on the Packers' 1943 team, then signed his contract. A hunting accident in high school kept him out of the military.

Lambeau signed Walter Gudie, a running back who once played at Wisconsin. Gudie was part of the Packers' pre-season eastern trip in

1943, but had commitments at a grocery business in La Crosse, Wisconsin, and didn't play during the season.

Next came signed contracts from tackle Milburn (Tiny) Croft, a two-year veteran from Ripon College who was working at a Green Bay cheese plant, and the anticipated agreement from Henry (Babe) Webb, the running back who had committed to the Packers in 1942 and 1943, but never could get transportation from Hawaii. Now living in Texas, he planned to finally make the trip to Green Bay.

Lee Joannes

Don Clark, a tackle from St. Mary's of Winona (Minnesota), and Dick Bilda, a running back from Marquette University, were next to send in signed contracts. And no bigger signing was the one that came from eleven-year veteran back and blocker Joe Laws a few days later.

Before the month ended, Lambeau received a signed contract from former Florida running back Paul Duhart, who had entered the army prior to his senior year in college and was recently honorably discharged.

While all this was going on, plans were being made to launch a season-ticket campaign. There were nineteen Green Bay firms represented when the Association of Commerce's industrial section met with Lambeau and Packers president Lee Joannes to organize the sale of tickets in the plants. It would lead up to the one-day, citywide sale of season tickets on August 23.

***

(The following war updates were provided by Major John M. Walter in his role as the orientation and communications officer at Camp Wolters in Mineral Wells, Texas. He wrote the daily war updates for the base and included them in his personal diary.)

July 1, 1944 - Great armored battle being fought south of Caen as Germans hurl in reserves ... Allies are driving toward the One river ... Germans are in headlong retreat up the west coast of Italy, being 20 miles from Livorno and 27 miles from Pisa ... The battle for Saipan is the costliest of the Pacific war to date ... Hengyang appears falling to the Japs ... Chinese are driving from Mogaung in effort to reopen the Burma road ... Soviets capture Borisov, Diana and Slutsk; they're 30 miles from Minsk.

July 6, 1944 - Hitler hurls in his reserves against the Soviets, but evacuates Kowel as the Reds bear down on Vilna ... a new offensive is under way south of the Pripet marshes ... U.S. troops are fighting in the streets of La Haye ... 5th Army is 13 miles below Livorno, where the Germans are preparing for a bitter stand ... they're mopping up the Japs' last corner on Saipan ... Gen. de Gaulle is expected in Washington tomorrow ... Our subs sink 26 more Jap ships ... Second airdrome is taken on Noemfoor ... Chinese still holding at Hengyang.

July 9, 1944 - British fight into suburbs of Caen in Normandy ... U.S. troops attacking on west take St. Jean de Daye ... Soviets battle way into Vilna ... Zhukov launches offensive between Kowel and Lwow, and is 45 miles southeast of Brest-Litovsk ... 5th Army is 10 miles below Livorno, with the capture of Rosignano ... the French are 21 miles south of Florence ... Desperate Jap counterattack on Saipan is broken up with heavy losses to the enemy; it's Bataan in reverse ... Chinese recapture Liling in Hunan province ... Roosevelt and de Gaulle are meeting at Washington.

July 15, 1944 - Yanks are within 2,000 yards of St. Lo ... Soviets launch drive against Low, 30 miles away ... in the north, they're less than 20 miles from East Prussia ... Axis envoys quit Turkey ... Tokyo announces survivors of the last B-29 raid have been executed ... Renewed U.S. air raids on Guam ... 5th Army is three and a half miles from Livorno, and 9 miles from the Arno river ... Japs trying to break out of Weak in New Guinea ... Hengyang in China again is on the verge of falling.

July 20, 1944 - Tojo cabinet falls, and Kido is new premier at Tokyo ... Soviets cross Bug river in old Poland north of Lwow, and are within 100 miles of Warsaw ... British-Canadians push ahead on Normandy plain ... Munich is given heavy aerial pasting ... Americans occupy Livorno, while Poles in Italy, capture Ancona ... Guam is bombarded for 15th straight day ... U.S. subs have sunk 17 Jap ships in past 30 days.

July 22, 1944 - Appeal over German radio for officers to rise against the Gestapo ... Report that von Rundstedt, von Brauchitsch have been killed by Nazis; also List and von Mannstein ... many indications of growing revolt ... U.S. troops swarm upon Guam; the invasion goes well in early stages ... Soviets cross Bug on 37-mile front, advance on Lublin plain ...they are 12 miles from Chelm ... Ostrov falls, and noose tightens around Lwow ... Bad weather bogs down Allies in Normandy ... American patrols in Italy probe German line across Arno ... British are pushing Japs out of India, and Nips are surrendering at Myitkyina.

July 24, 1944 - Hitler purge extends to eastern front; 8 field commanders are arrested ... Churchill says the war may end soon ... Soviets break into Lublin, 95 miles southeast of Warsaw, capture Pskov ... British take Emieville, 5 miles east of Caen ... 5th Army sweeps into Pisa; 8th is within 15 miles of Florence ... Marines threaten Agana, Guam capital, and invade Tinian island ... Chinese attacking Japs at Siangsiang, 60 miles north of Hengyang.

July 30, 1944 - Report Marshall Rommel killed in Normandy ... Americans advance 21 miles, getting 13 miles past St. Lo and 11 past Coustances ... Soviets are within sight of Warsaw ... they also are 20 miles from Gulf of Riga ... Orote peninsula on Guam is taken ...

17 more Jap ships sunk by U.S. submarines ... Flying bombs plaster London ... B-29's bomb Ashan and Tangku in Manchuria ... 8th Army is 5 miles from Florence.

July 31, 1944 - Soviets within Sulwaki triangle of East Prussia, with Cherniakhovsy the general ... Begramian is half way across Latvia ... U.S. ships are using Apra harbor on Guam ... Americans drive toward Avranches in Normandy as British launch new offensive below Caen ... New secret weapon is mowing the Japs down on Tinian ... 5 German divisions are defending Florence.

Packers Board of Directors

The Packers Corporation re-elected its officers at its annual meeting in 1944. The board included a nine-man executive committee, with Lee Joannes continuing as president, and twelve additional directors, all men with Green Bay business connections.

Executive Committee

Lee Joannes: President-treasurer, Joannes Brothers wholesale foods

Gerald Clifford: Attorney with Martin, Clifford, Dilweg, Warne

Emil Fischer: President, Atlas Warehouse & Cold Storage

Curly Lambeau: Head coach

Fred Leicht: President, Leicht Transfer & Storage

Henry Bero: Green Bay Police Department inspector

Henry Wintgens: Vice-president and general sales manager, Hoberg Papers

Andrew Turnbull: President and general manager, Green Bay Newspaper Company

Frank Jonet: Accountant

Directors

Milan Boex: General sales manager and assistant general manager, Northern Paper Mills

Edward Bedore: Buyer, Morley-Murphy Company

George Calhoun: Telegraphic editor, Green Bay Press-Gazette

Fred Cobb: President, Cobb's Sunlit Bakery

Leslie Kelly: President, Green Bay Food Company

Harvey Lhost: Sales manager, Hurlbut Company

Charles Mathys: Green Bay Glass & Paint Company

John Moffat: Manager, Wadham's Oil

John Paeps: Assistant manager, Murphy Supply Company

Ed Schuster: President, Schuster Concrete

Arthur Schumacher: Schauer and Schumacher Furniture

August Reimer: Reimer Meat Products

August 1944

Tail Gunner Joe

When students of political history look back at August 1944, they mark it as the month that first put Joseph McCarthy's name before Wisconsin voters statewide.

McCarthy put his name on the ballot for US Senate, the seat already occupied by Alexander Wiley. McCarthy wasn't expected to take Wiley's job, but as a fellow Republican, he was able to get exposure that would benefit him a couple of years later.

The *Green Bay Press-Gazette* trumpeted McCarthy whenever the opportunity presented itself. On the first of the month, it cited the letter of commendation awarded to McCarthy by Admiral Chester Nimitz as McCarthy was on home leave after sixteen months with the marines in the South Pacific.

Nimitz noted that the commendation was for "meritorious and efficient performance of duty in the Solomon Islands area from Sept. 1 to December 31, 1943."

McCarthy enlisted in the marines in 1942 as a private and was commissioned a captain in March 1943. He participated on numerous bombing missions as a gunner and was also credited with taking aerial photographs of enemy gun positions that contributed to subsequent strikes.

Home on leave, McCarthy toured the state prior to the August primary election. On one such trip to Milwaukee, he was praised by Shawano mayor Harry Meyer.

"Who, I ask you, has a greater right to sit in the Senate chamber and legislate for the returning servicemen than one who has gone through the hell of war?" Meyer said. "Capt. McCarthy's natural disposition and acknowledged capabilities to espouse the cause of the boys with whom he lived and fought and bled should serve as an appeasing assurance to the anxiety of mothers, wives and sweethearts that the welfare of these boys now and after the war, will be zealously championed."

Joseph McCarthy

The day before the mid-month primary election, the *Press-Gazette* used its opinion page to endorse both McCarthy and State Sen. John Byrnes, a fellow Republican who was hoping to unseat Democratic Congressman and former Packers star LaVern Dilweg.

Of McCarthy, the editorial read: "He is of commanding ability, just the right age and with a varied and manly career. He could ask some questions that would throw American boobs back on their heels or at least divulge to the public their prone and fawning position before the empire.

"He would help halt the unjust and needless sacrifice of the youth of the land while the people more interested sit on their haunches.

Local News Highlights

August 8: Many Green Bay residents had their first glimpse of the B-29, Super Fortress, when it flew over the city from 2500 to 3000 feet, flying north to south.

August 11: William Nielsen, who went to work as a telegraph operator for the North Western Railroad when he was 15, retired after 52 years as a dispatcher for the railroad.

August 15: Horse thieves broke into the fairgrounds stables and stole a large bay trotting horse that weighs 850 pounds.

August 23: The county has received five bids to erect sundecks at the Hickory Grove sanatorium south of De Pere. The facility also houses the mentally insane.

"He would help create an honorable and an upright foreign policy willing to do our full part even a few percent more, never to carry the load for shirkers but to make them carry it instead."

McCarthy before McCarthyism.

When the votes were counted, Wiley doubled McCarthy's total statewide - 131,548 to 66,994. But in Brown County, it was Wiley 2,576 to McCarthy 2,045. More importantly, McCarthy got the exposure he needed.

Residents continued to be called on to contribute to the war needs. The production staff of the American Red Cross made another appeal for odd lengths of yarn. It received a request from army and navy hospitals for more slippers like those on display in the Reiss Coal company office window in the Northern building. The slippers were made from rags and yarn scraps.

Housewives who wished to get the second half of their extra canning sugar allotment needed only send a card or letter to the Brown County war price and rationing board asking for the second ten pounds for each person whose name appeared on the original application.

An announcement was made that the Green Bay navy recruiting substation led all state navy recruiting substations in number of enlistments during the month of August.

The establishment of a rehabilitation and education center in Green Bay within the next three or four months was announced. It would be designed to help returning disabled veterans.

Green Bay retail stores joined stores in numerous other cities in the United States by saying they will be closing on VE-Day. A system had been set up whereby all retailers in the city who wish to be notified would be warned within a few minutes after an authentic report of surrender or armistice with either Germany or Japan was received here.

And there was wartime entertainment. The Milwaukee Chicks and Kenosha Comets, members of the All-American Girls Professional Baseball League, scheduled two games in Green Bay in late August.

***

Lambeau continued to sign up players for the 1944 Packers season. Contracts came in daily ahead of team workouts that would start the third week of the month. Most significant were the contracts of blocking back Larry Craig, linemen Bill Kuusisto, Buford (Baby) Ray and Paul Berezney, and fullback Ted Fritsch.

When the team gathered at Joannes Park for its first workout, Lambeau had thirteen veterans and seventeen new players. More than 400 people lined the sides of the park to watch.

Lambeau also decided to hire Robert Conrad as a full-time scout since Conrad had been doing some scouting for him in previous years. And at the team's annual stockholders meeting, longtime president Lee Joannes was renamed president for his fifteenth year.

To some, the Packers were a favorite as the season approached, even to far-away observers.

"The Green Bay Packers will be the team to beat this fall if Lambeau can talk Don Hutson and Buckets Goldenberg into playing again,"

Packers players participate in the first practice of summer training camp at Joannes Park, August 21, 1944. Coach Curly Lambeau welcomed thirty players to camp, more than half of whom were new to the roster. (Green Bay Press-Gazette photo)

wrote Red McQueen of the *Honolulu Advertiser*. "Without Hutson, the Packers will lose much of their color and gate attractiveness."

Getting significant publicity throughout the month was the growing possibility of competing pro football leagues. One was the United States League that was being promoted by Pittsburgh industrialist Roland Payne and another was the American league that was starting to stir interest on the West Coast.

This prompted the NFL to take a stand against the new leagues poaching its players. George Strickler, publicity director for the NFL, sounded the warning.

"Any National player who accepts a contract with any other league will be ineligible to play in our league for five years, and none of our teams can play another team which has on its roster such a player," Strickler said. "For older players, it may end their careers so far as the National league is concerned."

George Marshall, owner of the Washington Redskins, then suspended Dean McAdams after it was reported that he signed with the Seattle Bombers of the West Coast league.

NFL commissioner Elmer Layden tried to quell the competitive tension.

"You can't just assume a league," he said. "Every day I hear or read of one league or another being formed here or someplace else, but that still doesn't bring a league into being. I'm afraid it's impossible to discuss intelligently a thing that doesn't exist. If another Eastern league is organized and operates a season or two, then will be the time to give consideration."

The issue didn't impact the Packers or any of its players.

Instead, the annual season-ticket drive was the center of attention. The Packers teamed with the Association of Commerce to conduct a one-day drive in businesses and industrial plants, with eighty volunteers first sharing a breakfast at the Beaumont Hotel and then hustling to sell tickets.

At the end of the day, 1,054 season tickets were sold.

***

A massive crane at the C. Reiss Coal Company blew over in a storm less than a week before training camp opened for the Packers, August, 16, 1944. (Green Bay Press-Gazette photo)

The end of the month was time for the Brown County Fair, and while it drew the usual attendance and livestock entries, there was evidence of the war's impact. Absent were the usual machinery and appliance exhibits because of the work shortage. But very evident were the presence of captured German military artifacts, including a wrecked tank and a machine gun that was on display in the Exhibition Hall lobby.

While the community prepared to enjoy the annual county fair, the Sullivan-Wallen American Legion post was deciding what would go into the 5,000 Christmas boxes that would be sent to men and women from the area in the armed forces. As a list of recipients was being prepared, the legion announced the contents: two pounds of candy, one pound of fruit cake, nine ounces of peanuts, a shaving stick, lip ice, two bars of soap, pencils, twenty-five sheets of stationery, twenty-five envelopes, and a toothbrush.

***

Opinions were in front of the *Press-Gazette's* readers daily.

American Casualties
August 1, 1944

The cowled figure of Death has already claimed 63,000 youths in our armed forces. But there is another figure, more vague and uncertain but with a high percentage of mortality known as Missing in Action which accounts for nearly 50,000 more.

As Things Go in France
August 11, 1944

Our lightning dash across Brittany brought into our hands nearly or about 10,000 square miles of territory and some badly needed ports. Say what one may, our hold in Normandy was uncertain and precarious.

It was one thing, and not easy, to make a landing in force on the continent. It was another thing, and still more burdensome, to obtain enough territory and with it the invaluable shelter from the sea to insure the safety of the original landing.

Truth, War and Empire
August 19, 1944

For weary year upon weary year, both the Associated Press and the United Press, our two greatest news gathering agencies, have made a rigid and persistent fight for freedom of world news.

The importance of this battle against backward influences is better understood by global students than by most residents of inland America. For every year more than a billion people around the globe read no news that is not altered or twisted for them even as the potter shapes his planet of clay.

Farm Tenure Objectives
August 22, 1944

Any alert American knows that the economic problems that will come with the conclusion of the war and the reversion to an economy of peace will test the mettle of the country. It should be possible for qualified farmers to become owners or centers of farm units that will prioritize an equitable reward for intelligent management, necessary labor input and the use of necessary capital.

Paris and the French Problem
August 26, 1944

It was fine psychology for the American command to give the French troops with them the order to bypass and be the first to enter their historic capital in triumph. It was a delirious night for Parisians.

Today, France should have no greater ambition than to shoulder as heavy a part of the fighting load as she can possibly carry.

***

(The following war updates were provided by Major John M. Walter in his role as the orientation and communications officer at Camp Wolters in Mineral Wells, Texas. He wrote the daily war updates for the base and included them in his personal diary.)

Aug. 2, 1944 - Gen. Joe Stilwell gets his 4th star ... Nazis burn and demolish Warsaw as Reds drive into suburbs ... land communication is cut between East Prussia and the Baltics ... Kaunas is taken ... President Ryti of Finland resigns and Baron Mannerheim takes over ... Turket break with Axis rumored near ... U.S. gains 10 miles in two directions from Avranches ... Germans are defending Florence bitterly ... Organized Jap resistance on Tinian ends ... Chinese hold inner defenses at Hengyang.

Aug. 8, 1944 - Powerful American and Canadian columns surge toward Paris ... Yanks reach Le Mans ... British breach line south of Caen ... Allies are 100 miles from Paris ... Reds attacking between Warsaw and Krakow ... Konev's 1st Ukrainians are 30 miles past the Vistula ... Indian troops advance through mountains north of Arezzo in Italy ... Situation at Florence and Pisa unchanged ... Premier Koisi warns Japs of grave dangers ahead.

Aug. 13, 1944 - Americans push south beyond Loire river ... heavy bomb attacks on Mediterranean coast of France ... Germans throw reinforcements into potential trap below Caen ... Allied movements in north France are secret but on a stupendous scale ... Germans have withdrawn completely from Florence ... Zakharov's 2nd White Russian Army gains 6 miles through forts northeast of Warsaw ... reaches Biebrza river marshes ... in Baltic, Soviets gain toward Memel and Liepaja ... British bayonets chase last Japs from India.

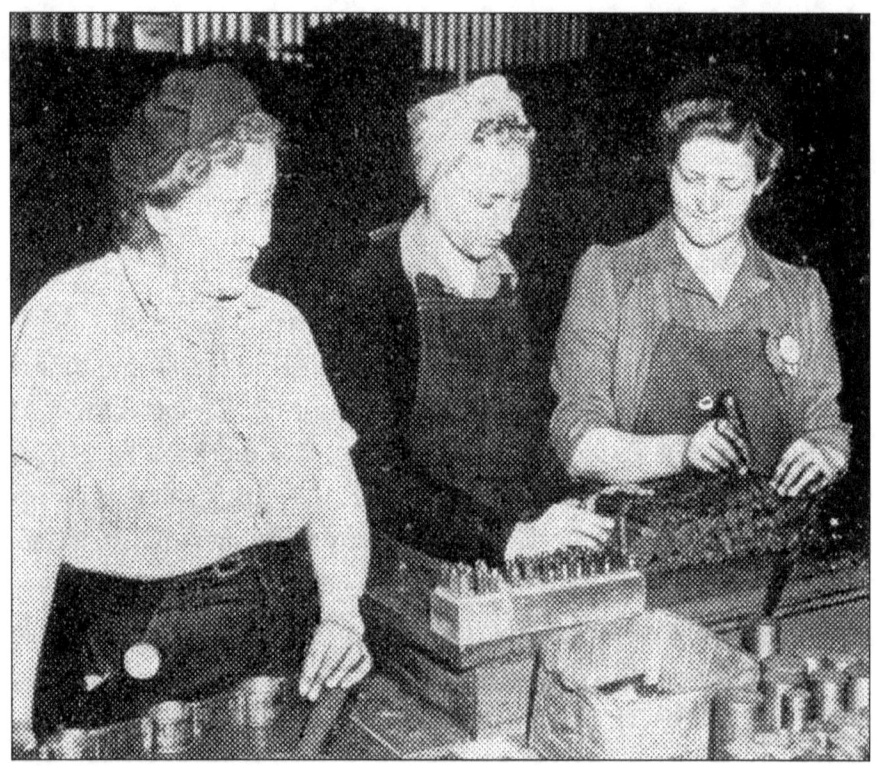

This photo from The Manitowoc Company's spring 1943 employee newsletter shows (from left) Irene Porter, Judy Pilster and Anne Nielsen with a caption reading, "These girls are doing a man's job in the Electric Shop." (Photo courtesy of University of Wisconsin-Green Bay Archives)

Aug. 18, 1944 - Patton's 3rd Army mops up around captured Orleans ... Vendome also has fallen, and that isolates the city of Tours ... the Petain-Laval government has fled Vichy ... the German radio announced that Patton's armor is 12 miles from Paris ... Canadians capture Falaise ... Allies are 35 miles inland in southern France ... they are 10 miles from Toulon ... 3rd White Russian Army (Cherniakhovsky) is attacking along East Prussia-Lithuania frontier ... Halmahera sharply attacked by Allied bombers ... Bulgaria is making loud peace noises.

Aug. 21, 1944 - Paris is flanked on two sides as Americans cross Seine river ... patriots are reported fighting in streets of the city ...

British near Lisieux along the coast ... Americans advance patrols are in Versailes and Fontaine-bleau ... Seventh Army in southern France is sweeping westward toward the Rhone valley, and are fighting at Aix-en-Provence ... French troops are three miles from the naval base at Toulon ... Twenty consecutive German counterattacks around Warsaw have been broken up by the Soviets ... there is severe fighting west of the Vistula river ... Germans penetrate Red lines before Riga in Latvia ... Soviets drive toward Ploesti oil fields in Romania ... Industrial targets around Yawata on Kyusha island of Japan are hit hard by fleets of B-29s ... under attack were the cities of Moji, Kokura, Yawata and Fukuoka.

Aug. 23, 1944 - Fifty thousand French patriots rise to overthrow German rule in Paris ... Gen. Patton's sweep southeast is gaining speed in a drive at the German frontier ... Sen has been liberated, and the Americans are approaching Troyes ... Seventh Army reaches Grenoble in advance from the south ... French continue encirclement of Toulon, and approach Arles northwest of Marseille ... Soviets capture Iassi in advance toward Ploesti oil fields in Romania ... in the north they have established a 37-mile bridgehead along the south bank of the Bug river ... 135 tons of bombs are dropped on Jap base at Halmahera.

Aug. 26, 1944 - German commander of Paris surrenders ... Allied reinforcements are pouring into city ... Gen. de Gaulle establishes his headquarters there ... on 200-mile front, American, British and Canadian troops advance toward Belgium and Germany ... Americans cross Marne east of Paris and reach Reims ... they have entered Troyes and are 120 miles from German frontier ... Allies smash toward Lyon in Rhone valley ... Avignon is liberated ... they are within short artillery range of Nice and nearing the Italian borer ... England reports a lull in the vicious robot bomb attacks ... Bombers hit Dutch Celebes ... Soviet troops sweep through Galati gap in Romania, are 100 miles from Bucharest.

Aug. 29, 1944 - Patton's forces sweep across Marne on 50-mile front, are 18 miles from Compaigne, and reach Chateau-Thierry ... Soissons is 20 miles away ... British and Canadians bear down on rocket gun coast ... in south, French cross to west bank of Rhone in two places, attacking Germans around Montelimar ... Nimes is in French hands ... The Fourth Republic is established in Paris ... Soviets pour through passes of the Carpathian mountains onto the plains of Transylvania ... they have captured Buzau and are within eight of the Ploesti oil field derricks ... Sulina is occupied along the Black sea ... Eight Jap ships sunk by aerial action in Dutch East Indies.

September 1944

Football

The war began its sixth year. Communities like Green Bay were becoming accustomed to reacting and adjusting.

One adjustment involved Labor Day. While some war-related plants would continue to be in operation on the holiday, there would be no traditional parades, baseball games or picnics planned in the Green Bay area. A Sunday afternoon concert at Bay Beach was the only public event scheduled.

No sooner had the Labor Day weekend ended when the US Employment Office in Green Bay got permission from the Kraft and Shefford cheese companies to recruit their women employees for evening work in local canneries. Tons of food was piling up at a rapid rate, so women would be asked to work four-hour evening shifts.

The need was there because the schools were reopening for the fall and many high school students who had been working the fields and factories were returning to school. School officials expected a lower high school enrollment in the Green Bay schools though, because many students were going to take advantage of the paychecks in war-related plants and put off education for the time being. Courses on most subjects were set up in a night school curriculum to help students keep up with their studies.

Two weeks into the month, the labor shortage at the Larsen cannery was abated somewhat. But officials of the Larsen Company said they believed that more rural women could be obtained to ease the labor situation in Green Bay canneries if more convenient means of bus transportation could be made available.

Plans for twenty-four-hour memorial services to start on the announcement of Germany's capitulation were formulated at a meeting of the Veterans of Foreign Wars. It included a request that all tavern keepers close during the services.

Trainees were being sought for enrollment in the US Maritime Service river pilot school in St. Louis. Anyone thirty years old and older or anyone under thirty and classified 1-C or 4-F was eligible.

Brown County was nearing completion of a county-wide harvest of milkweed, which was vital in the making of life jackets for servicemen.

It was announced that returning servicemen who applied to the Green Bay YMCA within one year after their discharge from the service would be granted three months use of the facility at no cost.

And five town of Preble tavern keepers were bound over in municipal court on charges of selling drinks after 1 a.m. The investigator for the state beverage tax commission testifying in the case was a navy veteran who was wounded while serving in the Pacific on the aircraft carrier *Hornet*.

***

It was closing in on the presidential election, and efforts increased to get ballots to servicemen and service women. Relatives and friends were being sent postal cards and urged to fill them out with names and military addresses of those in the armed forces so ballots for the November 7 election could be sent out.

One Green Bay veteran sent a letter to the Association of Commerce to say he received some of the cigarettes that were part of a *Green Bay Press-Gazette* collection the previous fall. He got the smokes when he

Local News Highlights

September 1: The large turnout of prospective freshmen at an organization meeting at the courthouse indicates that enrollment this fall at the University of Wisconsin Center in Green Bay will exceed last year's total.

September 6: An 11-year-old west side boy admitted to stealing three automobiles and ransacking at least a dozen others. He told police he drove one of the cars all the way to Wausaukee and hour north of Green Bay and back.

September 12: Packers ticket director Ralph Smith said rumors that the upcoming Packers-Bears game is already a sellout are untrue and pointed to the ticket racks at the American Legion ticket office. Tickets were still available for $2.40, $1.80 and $1.20.

September 16: Movie options for area residents included "Bathing Beauty" starring Esther Williams and Red Skelton at the Bay Theater, "Show Business" starring Eddie Cantor at the Orpheum, "Pin Up Girl" starring Betty Grable at the Strand, and "George Washington Slept Here" starring Jack Benny at the West.

September 25: FBI investigators visited Green Bay in search of women aged 17 to 35 who might be interested in applying for a position with the agency in Washington D.C. Shorthand and typing experience are not required.

aided the recapture of Guam.

And copies of the official government booklet outlining the rights and benefits of discharged veterans of World War II had been mailed to all area veterans discharged before September 1.

People, Leaders and War
September 1, 1944

William Shirer, unrelenting foe of Nazism and all its works, says that on the eve of the unprovoked attack upon Poland the German people were as a whole very much opposed to the Nazi plan and openly expressed their hatred of war. After the amazing successes of German arms against Poland and the overwhelming of the powers to the west, however, he sensed a changed feeling, a support of the master race idea and a confidence that Hitler and his associates were, after all, on the right track.

Truman Hugs the Myth
September 8, 1944

The gist of Senator Truman's acceptance speech was that the peace and security of the world depend upon Mr. Roosevelt's election to a fourth term. That is the party line at Washington and Mr. Truman is going to stick to it. We wonder if he ever considered what would happen to the peace and security of the world if the President were to die tomorrow. Would the world come to an end?

Draft Evaders - Up or Down?
September 12, 1944

The Senate has passed a bill to deprive certain classes of draft evaders of their citizenship. This action appears to be just. The nation should have little time for him who will not wear its uniform when called upon to do so.

A National Responsibility
September 13, 1944

All over the country today there is avid talk of "postwar planning." There are a thousand "postwar" programs and plans, some of them whimsical, some of them valid. Devote some thought in what has been called the nation's No. 1 postwar job - soil conservation.

How Long Can a Man Fight?
September 22, 1944

Questioned separately before returning them to their lines, the German nurses captured early in the invasion at Cherbourg responded in similar vein to the inquiry as to who will win the war. "Germany is tired and you are fresh," was the burden of their comment.

Today we are confident that the Reich is collapsing, but it might be of more importance than we seem to think were we to ascertain the direct causes for that collapse. Modern war, it appears, imposes too great a burden of filth, horror, stench and renders noise for the human machine to tolerate that long without serious impairment.

The Mockery of the Indispensable Man
September 26, 1944

Mr. Dewey is not indispensable. Mr. Roosevelt is not indispensable. Those who would make such a claim for either are hardly struggling to deal with reason. Instead, their appeal is to the frozen mind.

Were either man to be removed from this earth's activities, he would immediately be supplanted by another.

***

Now it was football season, and the Packers were about to make news that would help carry them to the next level.

Lambeau was closing in on a key commitment as the team road the train toward Baltimore for an exhibition game against the Washington Redskins. Don Hutson, who was on record saying 1943 was his last season as a player and who was now a full-time assistant coach for the Packers, was close to signing up for another season playing the game he had helped to redefine in his first nine seasons. Whether it was the shortage of capable pass receivers on the team's roster or his own realization that he just wasn't ready to give up the competitive excitement of the game, Hutson signed to keep playing.

It would prove to be pivotal for a team with title aspirations. Hutson's decision to keep playing would help to define the 1944 Packers season.

The Packers played three games in the first eleven days of the month, none of them counting on their record. The first was a 20-7 loss to the Redskins and quarterback Sammie Baugh with the Redskins getting the services of former Notre Dame star Steve Bagarus, who was on furlough from the navy.

Bagarus was Baugh's favorite target in the game and had most observers predicting a stalwart career for him after the war. He would play two seasons with the Redskins and two more with the Los Angeles Rams, but his impact never lived up to expectations.

Ted Fritsch scored the Packers' only touchdown and the Redskins tallied twice in the fourth quarter to win before 44,000 people at Baltimore's Municipal Stadium. Hutson didn't play.

Russ Davis, filing the story for the *Press-Gazette,* soothed his readers.

"Folks, don't be alarmed. Coach Lambeau has a great team in the making this season."

Bob Conrad, who returned to Green Bay after serving in the South Pacific, was back to scouting for the Packers. He was interviewed a few days after the Redskins game by Cy Kritzer of the *Buffalo Evening News* and took on the role of team promoter.

"You know Curly and how optimistic he is," Conrad said. "Well, I agree with him this year. I think we have something. In fact, I don't think we'll lose a single game from here to the end of the year."

Conrad pointed out that the Redskins started practice August 1, while the Packers didn't gather until three weeks later.

"Our men faded in that last quarter and were too tired to cover Sammie Baugh's passes," he said. "Hutson will play again. He couldn't quit if he wanted to. He's like an old fire horse when he hears that whistle."

From Baltimore, the Packers traveled to New York, where they were the guests of the Sampson Naval Training Center near Seneca Lake. The center had a football team coached by Lt. Jim Crowley, the former Green Bay East and Notre Dame star. The Packers toured the center, watched movies, and went bowling before defeating the center team 25-14.

Then they bussed to Buffalo to get ready for an exhibition game against the Boston Yanks. It was a one-sided game, the Packers win-

Halfback Lou Brock (16) carries the ball behind blocking back Larry Craig (54) and an unidentified teammate during the Packers' 14-7 victory over the Brooklyn Tigers at State Fair Park in Milwaukee on September 17, 1944. (Green Bay Press-Gazette photo)

ning 28-0 and only using Hutson to kick the four extra points.

The Packers then returned to Green Bay and got ready to host the Brooklyn Tigers (formerly called the Dodgers) in a season-opening game at State Fair Park in Milwaukee. The Packers had played the team just seven times previously and won all of them. Lambeau settled on twenty-one veterans and seven newcomers for his final roster.

The game – played before 12,994 in searing heat – was an endurance test for players and spectators. The visiting Tigers set a league record with twenty-two penalties for 168 yards and had three of their players ejected. Center George Smith was kicked out after he removed his helmet and threw it at an official. Packers tackle Ade Schwammel was also ejected for fighting.

The Packers won the game 14-7 despite being outgained on the ground and in the air. Hutson caught a touchdown pass from Irv Comp, and Lou Brock ran for the other score after a blocked punt gave the Packers the ball at the Tigers' 17.

Ralph Trost, writing for the *Brooklyn Eagle,* took a shot at the officials, claiming they ejected the wrong player.

Fullback Ted Fritsch (64) finds running room around the left end as halfback Lou Brock (16) trails the play during the Packers' 14-7 victory over the Brooklyn Tigers to open the 1944 season. (Green Bay Press-Gazette photo)

"If the officials could leave the wrong player out of the game, they could have made other mistakes," he wrote.

There was another quirk connected to the game. The State Fair Park press box had just one phone connection to the sidelines rather than the customary two, which would have given each team a chance to communicate to the field. So the Packers used the phone in the first half and then switched to the other sidelines so the Tigers could have phone access for the rest of the game.

That set up a showdown with the Chicago Bears in Green Bay the following Sunday. As the game neared, there was no indication that the Bears' great quarterback, Sid Luckman, would be available to play. As soon as the 1943 season ended with another Bears title, Luckman enlisted in the US Merchant Marine and was stationed at its Sheepshead, New York, base.

But two days before the game, the Bears announced that Luckman had permission from his commanding officer to play football on weekends. He would come to Green Bay and face the Packers.

The game would be the fifty-first between the rivals, with the Bears winning twenty-six, the Packers nineteen, and five ending in a tie.

The game at City Stadium was memorable. The Packers dominated the first half and took a 28-0 lead. Comp threw touchdown passes to Lou Brock and Hutson, and ran ten yards for another score. Fritsch scored on a one-yard run.

The Bears rallied and eventually tied the game in the fourth quarter. With three minutes left, Brock broke loose around left end for forty-two yards and a go-ahead touchdown, and then Fritsch intercepted a Luckman pass and ran it in for another score as the Packers won, 42-28. It was the most points scored against a Bears team at that time in their history, and it was the first time the Packers had beaten the Bears in Green Bay since 1939.

When someone mentioned to him after the game that he had played well, Luckman said, "But it wasn't enough. In this league they pay off when you win – and we didn't."

Bears co-coach Luke Johnsos said it took Luckman awhile to get warmed up.

"He told us he couldn't get started in the first half," Johnsos said. "He was calling the wrong plays at times. A golfer can't be idle for three weeks and win a championship tournament. It's the same in football."

Co-coach Hunk Anderson said, "Green Bay has a better team."

Luckman was expected to begin sea duty and wasn't likely to play again until the Bears hosted the Packers in early November.

Packers tailback Irv Comp outraces Floyd Rhea (24) and Joe Carter (55) of the Brooklyn Tigers to the corner during the Packers' 14-7 victory on a hot September 17 day in Milwaukee. (Green Bay Press-Gazette photo)

A similar plan was in place for the Redskins' Baugh. He was notified by his Texas draft board that he would be reclassified 1-A unless he returned and worked at his ranch rather than just play football. Baugh planned to spend the weekdays at his Sweetwater ranch, then commute to the Redskins' game sites.

It remained to be seen what impact the lack of practice time would have for the two most dynamic passers in the league.

***

(The following war updates were provided by Major John M. Walter in his role as the orientation and communications officer at Camp Wolters in Mineral Wells, Texas. He wrote the daily war updates for the base and included them in his personal diary.)

Sept. 1, 1944 - American First Army of Lt. Gen. Hodges crashes into Sedan and is poised on Belgian border ... Patton sweeps through Verdun and reaches point 32 miles from Luxembourg ... Americans take Commercy to south, and are 70 miles from Saarbrucken ... British enter Pas-de-Calais rocket coast area ... Germans are in headlong retreat along 200-mile front ... Seventh Army is 48 miles below Lyon ... Five more Jap ships sunk in Celebes ... Palau in Carolines also attacked from air ... Jap thrust toward Heilin in China checked by Chinese ... Soviet army drives 35 miles past Bucharest to reach Danube river along Bulgarian frontier ... they are in action 10 miles northeast of Warsaw.

Sept. 4, 1944 - Finland is quitting the war, and all Germans must leave the country by 15 September ... Brussels has been liberated by British troops, which then struck northwest toward Ghent and the North sea ... U.S. forces cross into Germany near Luxembourg border ... Lyon is liberated by northbound troops of the Seventh Army, which is less than 144 miles from a junction with Allied troops of the north ... Soviets launch new offensive in Poland, 28 miles northeast of Warsaw ... they are 38 miles from Brasov in Romania ... Davao in Philippines bombed by 150 tons ... Japs resume drive toward Kweilin in Kwangsi province.

Sept. 8, 1944 - Along a 250-mile front, Allies close in on Siegfried line ... heaviest fighting takes place along Moselle river line between Metz and Nancy ... In Belgium, U.S. First Army is at outskirts of Liege; British Second Army crosses Albert canal, is 25 miles northeast of Louvain ... Seventh Army units capture Besancon in drive north, while others are 40 miles from Belfort gap in Germany ... British, American commando units are fighting in Yugoslavia ... Soviet armies throw bridgeheads across Narew river above Warsaw ... B-29s hit two industrial targets in southern Manchuria ... Jap bases on Mindanao and Celebes are bombed ... British Eighth Army is four miles below Rimini on Italy's Adriatic coast.

Sept. 11, 1944 - Capital city of Luxembourg, third European capital to be liberated in 19 days, has been occupied by United States troops of the Third Army ... Third Army is six miles from German border at Aachen ... British patrols cross Netherlands border in north ... there is house-to-house fighting in Brest ... Seventh Army reaches Dijon, and is 16 miles from Belfort ... Carrier planes deal Jap base at Palau a severe blow ... there also were heavy attacks on Celebes, Halmahera, Mindanao islands ... Japs roll toward Kweilin in Kwangsi province of China, and are 90 miles out ... Germany refuses to evacuate Finnish Lapland area ... Soviets are 83 miles from Crakow in Poland ... fighting continues along Narew river line northeast of Warsaw ... Reds are 25 miles from Broz partisan troops in Yugoslavia.

Sept. 15, 1944 - Powerful new pincers against Philippines is developing, as Infantry and Marines of the U.S. land on Palau, 560 miles east of Mindanao, and Morotai in the Halmaheras, 250 miles below the Philippines ... Allied troops in Germany are moving into the outer defenses of the Siegfried line ... Americans are within a mile of Aachen ... east of St. Vith, the Allies have pierced a segment of the line ... strong German counterattacks along the Moselle hold Lt. Gen. Patton's Third Army back, but gains are made against Nancy ... Mortar and artillery fire are raking Warsaw, as Rokossovky's First White Russian Army takes Praga, reaches the Vistula across from the capital ... farther north in Poland the Reds take Nowogrod, 15 miles below the East Prussian border ... in Transylvania, Soviets and Romanians are 13 miles from Cluj ... German attempt to take Finnish Hogland islands broken up by Finns, who now are expected to declare war against Germany.

Sept. 22, 1944 - British Second Army, against bitter resistance, fights its way two miles north of Nijmegen in Holland, attempting to relieve cornered Allied airborne elements around Arnhem ... the advance threatens the German Ruhr valley ... Brest finally falls to Allies ... big tank battle continues in Third Army sector around Nancy; 105 German tanks have been knocked out ... around Belfort, Allies gain near Lure ... Soviet troops sweep down mountain passes from Romania to fan out on Hungarian plain ... in Baltic area, Red advance continues toward Riga and Tallinn ... Soviets are crossing Vistula into Warsaw ... Hundreds of carrier-based planes pound Manila area in Philippines ... 110 Jap planes are shot down and 95 more destroyed on the ground ... 37 Jap ships sunk ... Japs capture Wuchow in Kwangsi province of China ... In Italy, Canadians and Greeks of the Eighth Army capture Rimini and fan out into the Po valley.

Sept. 25, 1944 - Trapped airborne units at Arnhem relieved by British Second Army, which then swing eastward and invades Germany ... Nazis have only a 25-mile escape route between Arnhem and the Zuider Zee ... Americans siege guns are pounding the German Rhine line along a 50-mile front ... Duren, between Aachen and Cologne, is under especially heavy attack ... Huge Soviet pincers, aimed at Budapest, is swinging through Hungary and Slovakia, one arm being 100 miles from the capital ... Tito's Yugoslav partisans defat Germans in Bosnia, capturing Banja Luka ... German position in Baltics worsens by the hour ... Americans are driven from Stolberg in Germany ... Japs have been dealt body blows by another heavy U.S. attack on central Philippines ... Tokyo says the Jap fleet is waiting to engage the American Navy with "almost uncontrolled enthusiasm."

Sept. 30, 1944 - British Second Army is making slow progress in push toward North Sea coast or Zuider Zee ... big guns of Cape Griz New have been silenced, and Dover may celebrate ... U.S. First Army is slugging its way deeper into Siegfried line, taking eight fortifications in one attack southwest of Prum ... Third Army is battling German armor between Metz and Nancy ... French improve positions north and west of Belfort, and are 10 miles from the gap ... German counterattacks slow Allied advance in Italy ... Soviets drive through Carpatho-Ukraine, are within three miles of Tatar pass ... in Hungary they reach Szeged ... Three more islands north of Palau are invaded by U.S. Marines ... Japs are 35 miles from Kweilin in China.

October 1944

Too Much Hutson

The *Green Bay Press-Gazette* had long ago established its reputation as a politically conservative newspaper, its editorial policy taking regular shots at Franklin Roosevelt's New Dealers. With FDR closing in on his fourth-term election, the newspaper cleared plenty of front page space for Republican nominee Thomas Dewey.

In the thirty-one days of October that preceded the November 7 general election, Dewey's name appeared in seventeen front page headlines and his vice-presidential running mate's name, John Bricker, was in five. Roosevelt's campaign warranted nine front page headlines in the month.

"Dewey Charts His Course to Reduce Taxes," "Dewey Assails New Deal Bid to Control All," "Dewey Pleads Italian Cause," "Dewey Outlines New Deal Ills," "Dewey Is Going After Ballots in Midwest Area," "Dewey in Friendly Praise for Wisconsin," "Dewey to Map Postwar Job Plans Tonight."

The *Press-Gazette* gave ample space to both the Republican and Democratic national committees for lengthy political columns on a Presidential Battle Page that was in print regularly during the month.

But three weeks into the month, it made its preference for Dewey very plain in a lead editorial:

"The people must struggle to decide earnestly and accurately whether Dewey or Roosevelt would likely contribute more to a lasting peace.

"Mr. Dewey was very much opposed to America getting into the war. Had he been nominated and elected in 1940, it is clear that we never would have entered it. In this sense he represents 75 percent of the people of this country who did not want to go to war, satisfied as they were that lasting peace was a mirage and that the death of our boys would be futile.

"But Dewey recognizes, as should all those who were opposed to war, that having been thrown into it we must unite ... For this task

Postal workers prepare more than 3,000 Christmas boxes for a special shipment to men and women serving overseas, October 14, 1944. (Green Bay Press-Gazette photo)

Local News Highlights

October 3: The Green Bay Park Board asked the city council for an appropriation of $50,000 to lay the groundwork for construction of indoor swimming pools at West and East high schools.

October 5: Two national publications - Education for Victory and Young Wings - printed book reviews submitted by students at Franklin Junior High School.

October 11: The state conservation office announced that public hunting grounds would be expanded in the Fox River valley as farmers and other land-owners begin to appreciate the program.

October 17: October 17 was the last day that the Green Bay Post Office would accept Christmas parcels to be sent overseas.

the advantages of Mr. Dewey over Mr. Roosevelt are so many and so evident the voters can hardly remain unconscious of them."

Also on the ballot in November was the hotly contested race for the Eighth Congressional District seat. The incumbent Democrat, former Packers star LaVern Dilweg, was opposed by Republican State Senator John Byrnes of Green Bay.

Byrnes, in a speech in Door County, said, "Opportunity and jobs for all after the war depends upon a Republican victory in November."

Although there was growing optimism that the war in Europe would end soon, there was also a growing list of area servicemen who were spending the duration of the war in prisoner-of-war camps. The Red Cross hosted about fifty people who were next of kin to these servicemen, providing a chance for families to share communications and see maps of the likely prison locations.

Green Bay banks reported a brisk business cashing war bonds despite the expressed hope of Secretary of the Treasury Henry Morganthau Jr. that bond owners would not present the securities "except in case of absolute necessity."

Ballots received from servicemen who were currently listed as missing in action were counted in the general election unless there was proof of their death, Wisconsin Secretary of State Fred Zimmerman said.

Christmas boxes to men and women overseas, 3,000 from Green Bay and more than 480 from De Pere, were sent on their way in a special mail train car.

Green Bay East students had a week to invest $3,000 in war savings stamps and bonds to win the privilege of having the school's name on a plaque attached to an Army Weasel, a reconnaissance truck used on D-Day in France.

Residents of Berlin, Wisconsin, decided they wouldn't change the city's name, but a campaign was started to put an emphasis on the first syllable so it would sound differently than the German capital. The city continues to call itself BER-lin rather than Ber-LIN to this day.

The Office of Price Administration regional director said OPA was starting a nationwide campaign to control the prices of toys and games ahead of the holiday season. The shortage of toys and games in 1943 had sent prices soaring.

***

There was plenty of football to provide brief distractions from political and economic concerns.

The Packers returned to State Fair Park in Milwaukee to host the Detroit Lions and ... well, *Detroit Free Press* reporter Truman Stacey saw it this way:

"The Don Hutson express roared through Detroit like a whistle stop," he wrote. "Hutson, though a marked man, had his day. The old Green Bay miracle man, in the Indian summer of his remarkable career, exerted himself only when a dramatic gesture seemed appropriate. The threat of his presence, however, was oppressive enough to unnerve the Detroit defense."

Hutson caught nine passes for 88 yards, but it was timely defense that sparked the Packers to a 27-6 victory. The Lions scored first and

The Packers easily handled the Detroit Lions in game two of the 1944 season, beating the visitors 27-6 at State Fair Park in Milwaukee on October 1. (Green Bay Press-Gazette photo)

got to the Packers' 1-yard line on their next possession with a chance to take a two-score lead. Frankie Sinkwich carried to the one on third down, but Charley Brock and Hutson tackled Bob Westfall back at the 4-yard line on the next play to end the drive. The Packers controlled the rest of the game, getting touchdowns from Paul Duhart, Fritsch, Comp and Hutson.

Lions coach Gus Dorais said, "If we'd gotten that second touchdown, things might have been different. We weren't the same ball club after that."

Harold Kahl, writing for the *Detroit Evening-Times,* thought an interference penalty on Sinkwich, who was guarding Harry Jacunski, played a pivotal role in setting up the Packers' first score and turning the tide against the Lions.

"Two movie cameramen, who had their finders dead-on the play, said they saw no interference," Kahl wrote.

Then, after the Packers reached the Lions' 17-yard line, Lou Brock was set to pass when the head linesman blew his whistle, causing most of the players to pause. But Duhart ran into the end zone and Brock hit him for the score. The official said the Lions were offside and the TD counted.

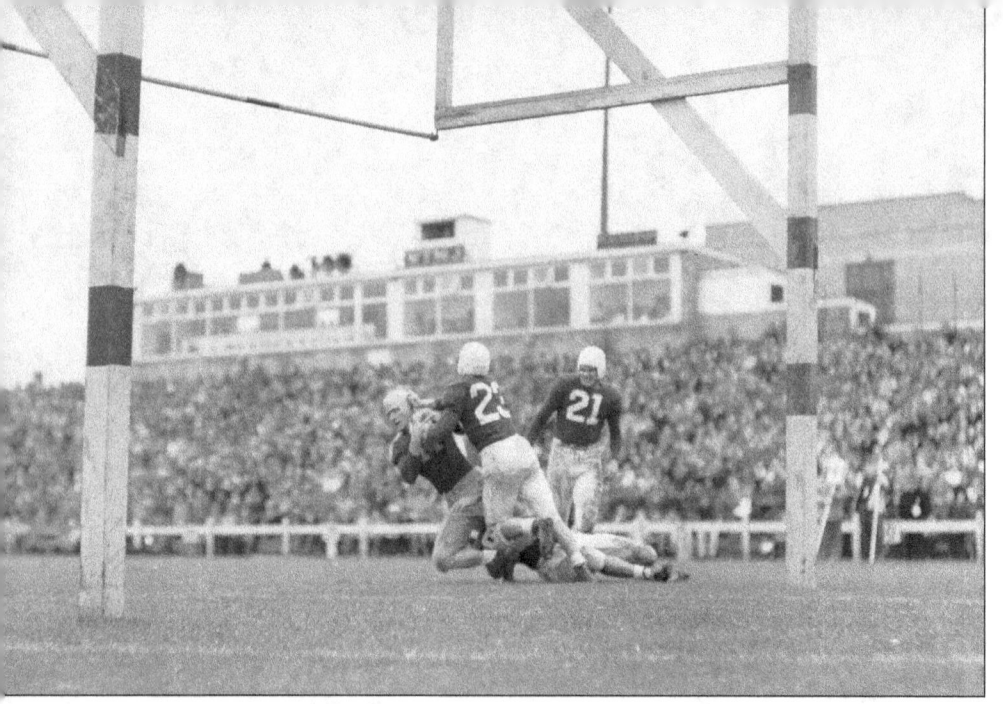

Don Hutson (left) is stopped just short of the goal line by Cardinals-Steelers defenders including Johnny Butler (23) during the Packers' 34-7 victory at Green Bay's City Stadium, October 8, 1944. (Green Bay Press-Gazette photo)

If Hutson was on the Lions' minds that Sunday, he certainly was on the minds of the players and coaches of the combined Cardinals-Steelers team that came to Green Bay the following Sunday.

Hutson caught eleven passes for 207 yards and the Packers breezed to a 34-7 victory in front of 16,525 at City Stadium.

"Too much Hutson," said Phil Handler, the losing coach. "I don't think you'd have much of a team without him."

Pittsburgh Press reporter Carl Hughes gushed:

"Among post-war plans for this Wisconsin football capital must be a life-size bronze statue of Don Hutson, the tall gentleman who makes the difference between Green Bay having an also-ran in the National Football League race and a champion. He didn't quite beat the Steelers-Cardinals single-handedly yesterday ... but probably could have had he wanted."

Wilfrid Smith, covering for the *Chicago Tribune,* wrote that Hutson "has radically altered defensive strategy in professional football by his speed and uncanny catches."

It could have been worse for the visitors as three Packers touchdowns were nullified by penalties. And one Cards-Steelers drive deep into Green Bay territory was stopped when Don Perkins intercepted a pass and returned it 83 yards for a touchdown that did count.

In the midst of this unbeaten streak, the Packers took a mid-week train trip to Nashville to play a benefit game against the Philadelphia Eagles to raise money for the 20th Ferrying Group of the Army Air Force. Its distinction was that it was the first professional football game ever played in the South.

Raymond Johnson, a sportswriter for *The Tennessean*, wrote: "Nashville fandom is most fortunate in having this big-time game. Since the first announcement that *The Tennessean* would bring the Packers and the Philadelphia Eagles to Nashville for a game, a num-

Don Perkins, a rookie out of the University of Wisconsin-Platteville, cuts outside for a big gain during the Packers' 34-7 victory at City Stadium over the Cardinals-Steelers, October 8, 1944. (Green Bay Press-Gazette photo)

Don Hutson (14) heads around right end behind a lead block by Tony Canadeo (3) during the Packers' 30-21 victory over the Cleveland Rams at Green Bay's City Stadium, October 22, 1944. Both men are members of the Pro Football Hall of Fame and the Green Bay Packers Hall of Fame, and are two of only six players to have their number retired by the team. (Green Bay Press-Gazette photo)

ber of southern cities have become highly interested in having a professional game. New Orleans, which a year ago wouldn't listen to an offer to have two of the top National league teams down there, now is anxious to have the play-for-pay clubs."

The Eagles won easily 38-13 as Lambeau rested most of his starters. Neither Hutson, Fritsch nor Comp played a single down.

Hutson later shed more light on the loss to the Eagles.

"Curly Lambeau and Greasy Neale (Eagles coach) had agreed to play principally second and third stringers," Hutson said. "Curly lived up to that agreement. Greasy saw a chance for the Eagles to get some favorable publicity by beating us and he used his good boys. That was all right with Curly, who not only wanted to get a look at a lot of goats we had on our squad, but also saw a future psychological advantage in such a loss if we had to meet the Eagles in the playoff."

The Tennessean's Johnson wrote, "The fact that Hutson didn't play was disappointing to the spectators, many whom came here from Alabama to see their former hero. They felt that Lambeau had given them the run-around."

Baby Ray, a native of Nashville who also attended Vanderbilt University in that city, was presented a trophy by students and teachers from Central High School, his alma mater.

Returning to league play, the Packers hosted the Cleveland Rams in Green Bay and had a bonus. Running back Tony Canadeo, now a corporal in the army and stationed at Fort Bliss, Texas, came home on furlough as his wife was giving birth to their son. Canadeo was in shape, having been playing with an army team, and he suited up against the Rams.

Tony Canadeo (3) carries the ball against the Cleveland Rams on a sun-splashed day at City Stadium on October 22, 1944. Canadeo, who was home on leave for the birth of a son, gained 107 yards on just twelve carries. (Green Bay Press-Gazette photo)

Packers fullback Ted Fritsch lowers his head to power through the line during the Packers' 30-21 triumph over the Cleveland Rams at City Stadium, October 22, 1944. (Green Bay Press-Gazette photo)

His presence was felt – he rushed for 107 yards on just twelve carries – and the Packers remained unbeaten with a 30-21 victory. The Rams made a game of it, scoring first on a 75-yard run by Tommy Colella, and the game was tied 14-14 at the half. But the Packers got touchdowns from Lou Brock and Ted Fritsch in the second half, and added a safety in the final minutes.

But Hutson was still the focus of the Rams' defense and the media.

Wrote John Dietrich of the *Cleveland Plain Dealer*: "The Packers will continue to ride high in pro football only as long as they have Don Hutson and the end is not far off, even though the great Alabaman today looks as good as ever. Without Hutson and without Canadeo, the Packers would have been no match for Cleveland today."

Rams coach Buff Donelli said the Packers "looked like a pre-war ball club and having Canadeo didn't hurt them a bit."

Canadeo's presence in the game was a surprise to the Rams, who didn't learn of his status until they reached Green Bay. By rule, Canadeo needed to get permission from his commanding officer, which he did, but Lambeau made no public comments about Canadeo's status during the week. A Chicago newspaper reported that Canadeo practiced secretly with the Packers the week before the game. His possible availability for the Rams game was first mentioned in the *Press-Gazette* two days before the game.

"The Rams would have appreciated the information," wrote *Plain-Dealer* sportswriter John Dietrich.

Their home schedule completed and sitting atop the West Division with a 6-0 record, the Packers traveled to Briggs Stadium in Detroit for their repeat game against the Lions. It was a 14-0 Green Bay victory on touchdowns by Fritsch and Laws, but the contest featured a scoreless second half in front of 30,844 fans.

The Lions didn't let Hutson score a touchdown but, as Bon Latshaw of the *Detroit Free Press* wrote, "Stopping Don Hutson wasn't enough."

The Packers weren't impressive in their victory.

"Although the Packers were never pressed in recording their ninth successive victory over a Detroit eleven," wrote Frank Kenesson of The Associated Press, "they were a disorganized outfit all afternoon, only once putting together any semblance of a sustained drive."

But the victory, combined with Cleveland's loss to the Bears, gave the Packers a two-game lead in the Western Division standings heading into November.

***

Opinions about the war and politics greeted *Press-Gazette* readers.

The Length of the War
October 4, 1944

Washington warns the country that it should expect the war to go about two years after the Nazis fall. What Washington should do is shock the country by telling it its honest opinion. From present indications the Press-Gazette has no reason to recede from the estimate it made when this war got under way, that it would go about ten years. The editor gets enough mail from men in the service detailing plenty of facts to substantiate that judgment.

The President and October Promises
October 7, 1944

Mr. Roosevelt said that he spurns the support of Communists just as he would of Fascists. He said the same thing in 1936. But after the 1936 election the Reds came to Washington virtually in droves. And Mr. Roosevelt's administration gave them jobs, permitted them to permeate the public service and often to poison it.

Moscow Swings Wildly
October 11, 1944

The Soviets took time out in the midst of war to bitterly flail the Vatican. It so happens that throughout the Christian world today, and quite irrespective of any particular sect, the Vatican stands high because it has extended its energies and influence for order and justice and peace and understanding.

MacArthur and After
October 23, 1944

Lauding General MacArthur has become an everyday affair in America and for good reason. His strategy in the Philippines is another superb example of his great ability as a supreme commander. For MacArthur aims to save lives. That isn't going to be the story on the continent of Asia. There we will meet millions upon millions of men willing to die for the emperor.

The Great Advantage of Experience in the Presidency
October 27, 1944

Now that America has suddenly become aware of Mr. Roosevelt's error in demanding Nazi heads before he had Nazi bodies in his power, now that it is equally apparent that thousands of American youths have been sacrificed upon the field of battle because of the President's inability to smother his vanity in striking a pose as an avenging crusader and without ordinary foresight as to the consequences, New

Dealers are almost running wild in the effort to diffuse the responsibility for the error by repeating from every side their opinion to the same effect.

***

(The following war updates were provided by Major John M. Walter in his role as the orientation and communications officer at Camp Wolters in Mineral Wells, Texas. He wrote the daily war updates for the base and included them in his personal diary.)

Oct. 2, 1944 - U.S. First Army launches new offensive below Aachen, aimed at Rhine ... Germans are counterattacking furiously against British Second Army near Nijmegen in Holland ... Third Army is pounding away but not gaining much ground; destroying a lot of armor, though ... Seventh Army gains near Epinal ... Channel port of Calais finally falls to Canadians, who promptly switch attention to Dunkirk ... Japs drive U.S. from big air base at Tanchuk in Kwangsi province of China ... British continue progress up Po valley in Italy ... British commando troops land on three islands south of Greece, including Kythera ... Soviet Second Ukrainian Army is 40 miles from Belgrade-Athens rail junction at Nis.

Oct. 5, 1944 - British air and seaborne troops swarm ashore on western coast of Greece, enter Patras, establish contact with enemy ... Soviet columns are within 10 miles of Belgrade ... U.S. First Army advances in three directions north of Aachen against fierce German resistance ... Germans drive American Third Army troops back to remote corners of Fort Driant before Metz ... 48-hour truce is in effect at Dunkirk ... Marines on Peleliu and Angaur have killed 11,000 Japs to date ... Japs are only six miles from Foochow in Fukien province of China, and capture Hungan, 31 miles northwest of Kweilin.

Grace Kaminski, Magdalen Meyer and Lillian Martin were among the pipe fitters helpers pictured in The Manitowoc Company's spring 1943 employee newsletter. The caption read, "The female gender in the Pipe Shop is no longer a novelty." (Photo courtesy of University of Wisconsin-Green Bay Archives)

Oct. 8, 1944 - Wendell Willkie, 1940 Republican presidential nominee and in my opinion the greatest living American, died today at New York ... First Army driving hard through 6-mile gap north of Aachen ... six German towns are swept up ... Third Army strikes in Luxembourg sector ... Soviets gain 28 miles on road to Budapest, bypassing Szeged ... Japs are bombed from Kuriles to Celebes.

Oct. 14, 1944 - Radio Tokyo reports that American guerrilla forces still are giving the Japs trouble in the Philippines, which is heartening news ... our B-29s give Formosa an unmerciful pounding ...

even the interior island of Leyte, Philippines, is attacked ... Chinese set Japs back 25 miles north of Kweilin ... First Army troops are near the heart of Aachen ... 700 dive bomber sorties were flown in one day ... British Second Army moving ahead on 30-mile front against Kleve, and is seven miles from German frontier ... French are making progress around Belfort ... 100,000 Germans are caught in the Soviets' Baltic trap ... Riga has fallen, or been liberated, whichever you prefer ... Hungary is in a state panic as Soviets near Budapest ... Athens is occupied by British, Poles and Greek patriots, and the Greek flag again flies atop the Acropolis ... Germans on Adriatic island of Corfu surrender ... Fifth Army in Italy captures height nine miles from Bologna-Rimini highway.

Oct. 17, 1944 - Germans launch five counterattacks around Aachen, all of them being crushed ... Cologne is hit by 2,100 planes, including 1,300 heavy bombers ... British enter Venray in Holland ... 606,000 German prisoners have been taken since D-day ... Budapest flares in open revolt as SS troops take over capital ... Soviet forces are within 50 miles of the city ... Reds and partisans are 23 miles from Skopje on the main escape route from Greece ... There is fighting in the heart of Belgrade ... That Jap 'naval victory' was a phony; the Nips fled without a fight as our fleet approached ... B-29s continue blasting Formosa and our Third Fleet plasters Luzon ... 14th AAF sinks Jap cruiser in South China sea.

Oct. 19, 1944 - Tokyo radio says warships of United States Navy have entered Leyte gulf in Philippines and are landing troops ... report is unconfirmed by U.S. ... heavy air assaults against Philippines continue ... Bad weather descends upon western front from North sea to Switzerland ... Germany admits Aachen is surrounded ... British Second Army gains toward Ruhr valley ... Huge Soviet offensive pounding against borders of East Prussia ... More British paratroops land in Greece ... cleaning out process proceeds at Belgrade.

Oct. 20, 1944 - United States Sixth Army invades the Philippine islands on Leyte, puts tens of thousands of troops ashore, liberates Tacloban, capital of the island ... Gen. MacArthur goes ashore in historic return ... huge ocean armada pounds the Philippine shores ... 13 hours after the initial landing no counterattack develops ... Soviets break German lines south of captured Eydtkau in East Prussia ...Nazis are driven from Debrecen, Hungary's third largest city, 116 miles east of Budapest ... Civil strife breaks out in Greece ... British shell Thebes, 32 miles northwest of Athens ... German suicide squads hold out in Belgrade ... Fall of Aachen is near ... Bruyeres, 12 miles northeast of Epinal, falls to Seventh Army ... British bog down along Venray-Amerika road in Holland ... Canadians gain near Breskens.

Oct. 23, 1944 - One hundred square miles of Leyte now held by U.S. invaders ... they oppose the infamous Japanese 15th Imperial Division ... Gen. MacArthur reinstates the constitutional government of the Philippines, with Tacloban as its capital ... Jap airmen are pinned to the ground ... Soviets mass along Norwegian borer ... they gain on both sides of Tilsit in East Prussia, where they have reached the Niemen river ... Reds slash 16 miles across northeastern Hungary in drive aimed at cutting Budapest-Vienna communications line ... British and Canadians launch vigorous drive to clear Antwerp supply line ... Canadians capture Breskens and Fort Fredrick-Hendrick ... British attacking near S.Hertogenbosch in Holland ... Third Army advances two miles east of Nancy ... Looks like a new revolution in Spain.

Oct. 25, 1944 - Major naval battle rages in central Philippines ... Japs lose large cruiser, plus extensive damage to other vessels, including a carrier sunk ... U.S.S. Princeton, a light carrier, is sunk ... Japs lose 150 land based planes ... Fifth B-29 raid of war is made on Kyushu, Japanese mainland ... further progress is reported from ground forces on Leyte in Philippines ... Soviets battle 25 miles inside

East Prussia along a 150-mile front from north of the Niemen river to the Suwalki triangle ... Insterberg is under artillery fire ... British and Canadian drives in Holland are held up by determined German resistance.

Oct. 27, 1944 - Today is 169th anniversary of the founding of the United States Navy, and the fleet celebrates its greatest victory in history - 10 Jap battleships, three carriers, 21 cruisers and destroyers, 190 planes sunk, shot down or damaged ... strait of San Juanico between Leyte and Samar is under full U.S. control ... 15 more villages on Leyte are liberated, and the land front extends 40 miles southward from Tacloban ... Scots troops enter Tilburg in southern Holland, as British land on South Beveland island in Schelde estuary ... Berlin predicts big Allied offensive in Metz sector ... Soviet armies in East Prussia are four miles from Gumbinnen, 65 miles southeast of Konigsberg ... Reds capture Mukacevo in Czechoslovakia.

Oct. 31, 1944 - Churchill, addressing Parliament, says the war in Europe is likely to continue until Easter ... S. Beveland island of Schelde estuary is under complete Anglo-Canadian control ... German 15th Army, under cover of heavy fog, is retreating north of river Maas in Holland ... RAF heavies drop 4,400 tons of explosives on Cologne ... Great tank battle rages between Tisa and Danube rivers in Hungary, with the Soviets 50 miles from Budapest ... Germans counterattacking heavily in East Prussia ... Relief of Gen. Stilwell from CBI theater at demand of Chiang-Kai-Shek stirs new controversy among the so-called United Nations ... Japs are in outskirts of Kweilin and Liuchow in Kwangsi province ... Jap casualties on Leyte to date total 24,000 to 3,200 for U.S. ... reinforcements continue to pour ashore ... Manila area bombed ... Battle of the Philippines cost Japs between 25,000 and 35,000 seamen and naval officers.

November 1944

Little Boys Always Come Home to Cry

Undefeated when the month began, the Packers traveled to Wrigley Field for their return engagement with the Bears. Green Bay was the last team to beat the Bears at Wrigley in 1941.

The Bears had little chance to overtake the Packers in the standings.

"This is about all the one-time masters of professional football are defending today," wrote Edward Prell of the *Chicago Tribune*. "Unless it's what they consider an unalienable right to smack down the Packers on sight."

The Packers fell to the Bears 21-0 in front of 45,553 fans at Wrigley Field on the first Sunday of the month. It was the team's first shutout loss in 73 games dating back to the 2-0 loss to the same Bears in 1938.

Bears co-coach Luke Johnsos was smiling when he entered the press box after the game.

"Who wouldn't grin when you've just beaten the best team in the league?" he said.

The Bears dominated in every statistic, 15-8 in first downs, 129-49 in yards rushing, and 182-97 in yards passing. Tony Canadeo played in the game, but didn't return to Green Bay afterwards, instead heading back to the Texas army base.

Hutson caught six passes, but his streak of scoring in forty-one consecutive games ended.

The Bears admitted 1,900 servicemen to the game free of charge and entertained fans at halftime with what a Chicago newspaper printed was "a football game between the Negro students at Washington Park school and the white boys from Columbus Park."

A guest of the Packers at the game was Mrs. Hal Van Every. Her husband, a former Packer who became a bomber pilot, had been shot down over Germany six months earlier. He was sent to Stalag Luft III prison camp and would be liberated the following April by General Patton's army.

It didn't take long for the Packers to get back to winning. They

Head coach Curly Lambeau (center) reviews plays with assistant coaches Eddie Kotal (left) and Richard (Red) Smith in 1943. Smith resigned that December and in November of the following year would be the focal point of a controversial article regarding the relationship between Don Hutson and former Packers quarterback Cecil Isbell. (Green Bay Press-Gazette photo)

Local News Highlights

November 2: Youths aged 16 and 14 admitted using powerful slingshots to fire pellets through the plate glass windows of the press box at City Stadium.

November 7: The Office of Price Administration and Rahr Green Bay Brewery settled on damages of $5,120 after OPA charged the brewery of overcharging for malt beverages.

November 11: The Green Bay office of the Smaller War Plants corporation said it had 26 different vessels such as motor yachts, schooners and motorboats that the War Shipping Administration wants to sell as surplus property.

November 20: Krambo Foods Store was selling Thanksgiving turkeys for 49 cents a pound, 47 cents for turkeys over 16 pounds.

---

went to Cleveland and dismantled the Rams 42-7, with Hutson and Joe Laws each scoring two touchdowns and Roy McKay playing his first game of the season and throwing two touchdown passes.

The victory kept the Packers' Cleveland record perfect, never having lost there since the Rams joined the league in 1937.

Cleveland Plain-Dealer columnist James E. Doyle summed it up: "Cleveland's previously rambunctious Rams caught the Green Bay Packers on a rebound from a shutout at Chicago. And so you know what they caught. The Rams were in the hands of a receiver early at old League Park yesterday. A receiver by the name of Don Hutson."

From there, the Packers took the train to New York City, then forty miles up the Hudson River valley to Bear Mountain, where they would encamp and practice in preparation for a game against the Giants at the Polo Grounds.

While the Packers were in the east preparing for their game, a story broke in a national magazine that stirred emotions and shed some light on former line coach Richard (Red) Smith's relationship with Lambeau.

Smith resigned as the Packers line coach in December 1943 after a conference with Lambeau. He made a statement at the time thanking the team's executive committee and fans, but didn't mention Lambeau.

Lambeau implied that Smith's resignation was influenced by his commitment to baseball and that the football coaching job would interfere. Smith was set to be an assistant baseball coach for the minor league Milwaukee Brewers and had managed the Green Bay Bluejays minor league team in 1941 and 1942.

Ray Pagel, the *Green Bay Press-Gazette's* sports editor, wrote that many fans called the newspaper to express their surprise at Smith's resignation, and he pointed out that Smith always seemed to have the respect of the players he coached.

New York Times columnist Arthur Daley wrote a story for *Collier's Magazine* in which he heaped praise on Hutson.

"For ten long seasons the smartest minds in football have tried devising ways and means of checking this supreme artist at catching passes. No one has done it yet.

Assistant coach Red Smith (right) handles the blocking sled for tackles Paul Berezney (left) and Baby Ray in this 1943 photo. (Green Bay Press-Gazette photo)

Don Hutson (left) and Cecil Isbell are either drawing pass routes in the turf or participating in a cheesy photo pose at City Stadium in 1941. The two men were the subject of a November 1944 magazine article in which the writer questioned how well they got along. (Green Bay Press-Gazette photo)

"Don is a specialist, a receiver beyond compare. Babe Ruth, Jack Dempsey, Bill Tilden, Bobby Jones and the other sports immortals have had rivals to threaten them. The cool and nerveless Hutson has no one within shouting distance of him and, what's more, he may never have. The chances are that he is the most extraordinary athlete football has yet produced."

Heady stuff and Packers fans certainly ate it up. But that's not what made the headlines. Daley's story included a reference to Hutson's relationship with former Packers quarterback Cecil Isbell (the current Purdue head coach), claiming, without naming his source, that the two athletes were not on speaking terms when they played together for the Packers.

Packers center Charley Brock was in his fifth season out of the University of Nebraska for the 1944 season. He was listed at six-foot-two, 207 pounds. (Green Bay Press-Gazette photo)

The news landed in Green Bay like a bomb and the reactions were immediate. Lambeau said he contacted Daley and learned that his source on the Hutson-Isbell relationship was Red Smith.

"I called Daley twice on the telephone while we were in New York to find out where he obtained the information," Lambeau said. "Daley twice told me it had come from Red. You can put me on the record as saying that I am thoroughly burned up about it. As a matter of fact, Isbell and Hutson are the best of friends and there is no truth to the statement that they were not on speaking terms. Don has visited Isbell's home and just this year sat on the Purdue bench at the Michigan game at Isbell's invitation."

Both Hutson and Isbell denied that there was a problem between them. Hutson called Daley, also.

"Daley was all apologies about it but he could have asked Isbell, me, or hundreds of others whether what he had written was true," Hutson said. "I can't understand why he would do that without checking the truth of the statements first."

Isbell said the same, adding that "Daley owes both Hutson and me an apology."

Lambeau fired back at Smith.

"Red Smith made trouble for us when he was here and we attempted to protect him," he said, without adding any details. "But when he violates the first principle of sportsmanship by giving out deliberate falsehoods, it is time to call a halt."

There was no record of anyone contacting Smith for a comment at the time.

But the fuss didn't end there. Smith sent a letter to the *Press-Gazette* and attached a letter he received from Daley.

Wrote Daley: "I did speak twice to Curly Lambeau although I never before knew that private conversations were subject to use in the public prints. The first time I spoke to Curly your name never was mentioned. The second time he specifically asked me if I had spoken to you. I told him that I had talked to many persons and had picked up considerable information throughout the many years. Apparently, Curly chose to jump to conclusions he wanted to jump at."

Smith, in his letter to the newspaper, wrote "I hope this will correct any idea that Lambeau misinformed the public about. Little boys always come home to cry and this time it is the coach and not the players. Again, Lambeau used his masterful art of twisting words and was not man enough to take a loss."

Two decades later, Smith lent his name to organizers of an annual sports banquet in Appleton in 1965.

No doubt, Smith got some satisfaction in 1944 when the Giants hosted the Packers at the Polo Grounds that third Sunday of the month.

It was a 24-0 Giants victory in front of the largest crowd (56,481) in the league season. The Giants limited Hutson to four catches for thirty-one yards and blanketed him throughout the game, intercepting three Irv Comp passes.

Russ Davis, filing his game story for the *Press-Gazette,* was direct. "Let's be rough about it," he wrote. "The Packers looked very poor."

"We bottled up Hutson because we made him go where we wanted him to go," said Giants coach Steve Owen.

With the game out of hand, Lambeau kept Hutson on the sidelines in the fourth quarter.

Lambeau said, "The Giants are always tough. And don't be surprised if we have to take 'em on again in the playoff. It's beginning to shape up."

Adding suspense to the game was a phone call Lambeau said he received at his room at the Hotel New Yorker after the game. The caller didn't identify himself, but told Lambeau, "Next time you play here in New York, don't train at Bear Mountain. Every one of your practices was scouted."

Told of the phone call, Hutson said, "It was possible. They were shifting to meet those new plays of ours ... and we hadn't run them off against any team in the league this year."

Despite the loss, the Packers clinched the Western Division title because the Detroit Lions beat the Chicago Bears 41-21. With their victory, the Giants kept their Eastern Division title hopes alive despite still trailing the Philadelphia Eagles by a game.

The scheduling quirk of 1944 had the Packers with just one more regular season game – at Comiskey Park against the combined Cardinals-Steelers team. The Giants and Redskins were scheduled to play on back-to-back Sundays in December, so the Eastern Division winner wouldn't be known for a while. There was even a chance of a three-way tie in the East, so coins were flipped to determine who would play where if that happened.

The Philadelphia Eagles held a slight lead over both the Giants and Redskins, but they were swamped by the Bears 28-7 the follow-

Don Hutson (left) addresses the crowd at State Fair Park in Milwaukee during Don Hutson Day ceremonies on October 21, 1945, the last of his eleven seasons with the Packers. Among those looking on is Dominic Olejniczak (right), mayor of Green Bay and future Packers president. (Green Bay Press-Gazette photo)

ing weekend. Both the Giants and Redskins won and were set to play their back-to-back series. If they split their series and the Eagles won their final game against Cleveland, Philadelphia would win the Eastern Division.

The Packers beat the Cards-Steelers 35-20 on the last Sunday of November with Lambeau resting many of his starters. But the losing coach, Phil Handler, bemoaned the fact that he didn't rest Hutson.

"I hope to live to see the day when we can play the Packers without Hutson," he said. "Without him today, the Packers would have been out of luck. He's a fine fellow and a great player, but I'd like to play that team when they didn't have him."

Hutson scored two touchdowns and kicked five extra points.

Knowing it would be three weeks before the championship game, Lambeau gave his players the week off, but insisted that they maintain their weight. He then made arrangements for the team to travel to Charlottesville, Virginia, to train for the title game.

Meanwhile, sports columnist Hugh Fullerton Jr. reported that former Packer Johnny Blood was organizing an army football team in China.

***

The month would fit into history books for providing the canvass to deliver the nation's first four-term president.

Many in and around Green Bay might have been presuming that the election between Roosevelt and Dewey would be a close one. For sure, the *Press-Gazette's* editorial page fed them that likelihood. Four days before the November 7 election, it hailed Dewey for what seemed a generous step on his part.

"Mr. Dewey returned to Albany and called a special session of the New York legislature to extend by two hours the voting time in the City of New York on Election day with the knowledge that all the advantage of such a law will inure to his opponent … That one act of Mr. Dewey may even defeat him, so hide-bound tight is the election becoming."

Four days before the election, the *Press-Gazette* reported that three national polls predicted a "Photo Finish" and that fifteen states were too close to call.

Of course, it wasn't even a footnote. Roosevelt won easily and by noon the following day was able to count 407 electoral votes to Dewey's 124, even though Dewey beat FDR in Wisconsin by 20,000 votes.

The election did send former state senator John W. Byrnes to Washington as the Green Bay Republican defeated incumbent Dem-

John W. Byrnes defeated former Packers star Lavvie Dilweg in the November 1944 Eighth Congressional District election. Byrnes would become a fixture in Congress, serving the district for twenty-eight years. (Green Bay Press-Gazette photo)

ocrat and former Packers legend Lavvie Dilweg by about 7,000 votes in the Eighth Congressional District race. Byrnes would hold the seat for twenty-eight years.

It was the major news event in the month, but another less-publicized event had long range impact on the community. The soil borings on land for the proposed new Brown County airport in Ashwaubenon showed that the land was suitable for an airport. The State Planning Board then signaled its approval and expected the Civil Aeronautics Commission in Minneapolis to sign off on it. The county's airport committee could then proceed to acquire the land before the options expired December 1.

Lining Up the "Merchants of Death"
November 1, 1944

The Democratic National Committee presents to the country some business men whom it claims support the fourth term.

We have no criticism of any person, in business or elsewhere, who has faith in the fanciful and frenzied proposal to bring prosperity to America by sending or keeping our millions of young men in foreign lands or erecting Pittsburghs all over the world. There may be a trace of business men who support this chimera but they are rare indeed.

What we are interested in is the way our Caesars are lashing into line the men who are making fortunes, fabulous fortunes, out of this war.

The Curse of the Third Term
November 6, 1944

Mighty and friendly, trusting and confident, with in thought, in literature, in science, this America of ours has drawn out over it by the princes of luxury who direct its course a glittering veil of the emptiest illusion.

And so today America is groaning as nearly 200,000 of her sons rot in sickened spots around the world. The Curse of the Third Term may be seen in the tear-stained eyes of 200,000 mothers and heard in the suppressed sobs of 200,000 fathers.

The Election and International Understanding
November 9, 1944

America continues to astonish the world. No doubt, when our foes heard prominent men criticizing our government they were heartened. But that, as every American knows, only indicated how densely ignorant they were of this country,

The election, the very fact that it was held and the comparative order that attended the casting of the ballots, is like the seal upon the bond another confirmation of American greatness and of its capacity for good.

Members of the Disabled American Veterans fire off an Armistice Day salute to mark the end of The Great War, or what came to be known as World War I, November 11, 1944. (Green Bay Press-Gazette photo)

Armistice Day
November 11, 1944

Last night the radio told by name of men in our front line in France who were at the identical place 26 years ago. But instead of the joy of victory we face today what may be a prolonged slaughter throughout the world.

We do not know anything better than to have the public recall on a day like this the causes, both individual and nationalistic, that made an enduring peace in 1918 impossible with the hope that such causes, even as they are already appearing, to predominate the coming peace, may be exposed and destroyed else the result of this war will merely parallel the last one.

The Fight in the Philippines
November 14, 1944

Gratifying as is the sinking of Jap transports trying to reinforce their Leyte army the bad part of the story is that the enemy succeeded in landing heavy supporting columns of men and equipment and have evidences the regular oriental unconcern about the thousands drowned.

Jap losses in manpower, to date, however much greater than our, will never seriously affect the war's course. Sorrowfully as we would consider them were we to suffer likewise.

The Training of American Youth
November 20, 1944

Of course, the President is right in urging congress to adopt a peacetime plan for the training of American youth.

For internally we have pretended that we could never go to war. But have always gone. And when we have made these weak and retreating pretenses we have thereby invited aggressive nations to attack others, confident as they were that we would never be able to get trim fast enough to prevent them.

The Fires Must Be Constantly Stoked
November 22, 1944

In the first ten days of this month, 83 million less in war bonds were sold than in a similar period last year. During those same ten days 71 million more of these bonds were cashed than a year ago.

This is an unpleasant looking record for the home front to make.

That Naval Victory
November 28, 1944

The American naval victory in Philippine waters was momentous enough to suggest the rather enthusiastic explanation which was issued by Washington.

The victory was necessary to make the Philippine campaign a success. It was of high spiritual value too. It reached out much farther than booming guns can ever reach

***

(The following war updates were provided by Major John M. Walter in his role as the orientation and communications officer at Camp Wolters in Mineral Wells, Texas. He wrote the daily war updates for the base and included them in his personal diary.)

Nov. 1, 1944 - Tokyo issues confused report about our B-29s attacking that city. If true, it is the first time our land-based planes have been over the capital, but presumably not the last ... Tokyo also claimed fresh Jap forces landed on Peleliu in the Palau group ... U.S. troops are driving up Leyte valley toward Carigara bay, where the 5,000 Japs remaining on the island are expected to make a last ditch stand ... American, British and Chinese forces in Burma launch new offensive ... Canadians in the Schelde estuary battle onto Walcheren island from S. Beveland ... steady progress is made in driving the Germans north of the Dutch Maas ... RAF makes two more heavy attacks on Cologne ... Soviets battle in streets of Kecskemet, 43 miles southeast of Budapest ... they are 115 miles from the Austrian border ... British reach Salonika area in Greece, and Nazis fleeing north turn westward into Albania ... some fun, hey kids?

Nov. 4, 1944 - Mighty Soviet forces roll into suburbs of Budapest ... Red artillery is pounding the capital ... a Soviet naval flotilla is sailing up the Danube to join in the attack ... In East Prussia violent German counterattacks drive wedges into Soviet lines around Goldak ... all of Baltic area has been cleared of Germans except small area around Liepaja in Latvia ... last Germans have been driven from Greece ... Advance of American First Army toward Cologne slows down before fierce resistance ... town of Schmidt is captured by U.S. infantry, but is lost in counterattack, dive bombers promptly wiping the town off the map ... British and Canadians on Walcheren island

Tony Walter

in Schelde estuary are pinned to their beachheads by withering artillery fire ... Polish, British and American troops are pouring across the Mark river in Holland ... Japs land seasoned troops on Leyte to reinforce their garrison ... Jap planes attack Third Fleet, damaging several ships ... Chinese fighting hard in Kweilin ... Recent B-29 raid on Rangoon caused extensive damage to rail installations.

Nov. 7, 1944 - Today is the 27th anniversary of the Soviet Union's October Revolution, and is the occasion of wild celebrating in Moscow ... Marshal Stalin took a swipe at the Japanese, calling them an aggressor nation and one of the world's trouble makers ... all Soviet frontiers now have been cleared of Germans ... Soviets make two attempts to cross Danube south of Budapest ... Jap radio reports B-29s on reconnaissance over Tokyo again ... Two columns of U.S. Sixth Army closing in on Jap positions at Ormoc in Philippines ... southern column is 12 miles out and northern 15 ... British capture Willemstad in Holland and Americans are inside Moerdijk ... British and Canadians take Middelburg on Walcheren island ... last Germans south of Maas river are being mopped up ... Hard fighting continues southeast of Aachen, with First Army slugging its way slowly through Hurtgen forest ... RAF pounds Coblenz and other targets.

Nov. 11, 1944 - There are 35,000 fresh Jap troops on Leyte island, and a savage battle for Ormoc is in progress ... seven Jap destroyers and three transports were sunk by air action ... U.S. B-29s attack Nanking, puppet capital of China ... British subs sink 45 more Jap ships, and U.S. subs bag six ... Japs continue to claim capture of Kweiling and Liuchow but Chinese are advancing toward Bhamo in Burma ... Soviet armies have driven wedge between Budapest and eastern Slovakia ... Red artillery pounds Germans in East Prussia, 300 heavy guns to the mile along a 95-mile front ... U.S. Third Army continue to roll across Metz plain toward German Saar basin ... three to six mile advances were made yesterday ... seven more miles of Moselle river are cleared of Nazis, and 15-mile hole in the Nazi defense sis punched below Metz ... 11 more French towns are liberated, including Chateau-Salins ... First Army locked in bitter battle in Jurtgen forest southeast of Aachen ... Prime Minister Churchill arrives in Paris for Armistic day review with Chief pf States de Gaulle.

Nov. 14, 1944 - Germans show signs of Abandoning Metz as Third Army throws ring of steel around fortress ... Americans are outflanking Fort Driant and have expanded new bridgehead across the Moselle ... one column of Third Army is a mile and a half from German frontier ... to the south, around Luneville, Allies advance in sailing snowstorm ... German battleship Tirpitz is sunk in Tromso fjord of Norway by British Lancasters ... 12,000-pound earthquake bombs did the stunt ... Soviets take Jaszapati, 45 miles east of Budapest, and have broken into Jaszbereny, southeast of the city ... Germans claim there is fighting at Verses, five miles south of Budapest ... Jugoslav partisans are fitting in streets of Stoplje ... 200 Jap troops invade tiny island of Ngeregong, eight miles northeast of American-held Peleliu ... Five Jap divisions are faced into defensive positions around Ormoc on Leyte as 1st Cavalry Division and 24th Infantry Division advance on the port ... Chinese troops in Iriwaddy valley are only two miles from Bhamo.

Nov. 18, 1944 - Third Army troops have driven into Metz from north and south ... Cavalry patrols of same army have crossed German frontier around Thionville ... French First Army is five miles from Belfort ... American Seventh Army is a mile from St. Die, which in turn is 35 miles from Bavaria ... American First Army has broken through defense bulwark before Ruhr, has captured Gressenich and is 26 miles from Cologne ... U.S. Ninth Army is moving east along a 20-mile front and has repulsed strong counterattack 15 miles northeast of Aachen ... British Second Army holds 10 miles of Maas river bank ... Four communications centers of northeastern Hungary, including Hatvan, are menaced by Red army advances, with Germans retreating along 100-mile front toward Bratislava and Vienna ... Jugoslav partisans are fighting within Tirana, Albania capital, and are nearing Zagreb, capital of Croatia ... 3,000 Japs are surrounded by 32nd Division in Ormoc area of Leyte ... 32nd yields no ground to several Jap suicide attacks.

Nov. 21, 1944 - French First Army reaches the Rhône, sends tank column rolling northward on west bank of river, which it holds from Besel to Colmar ... Belfort falls by storm to French colonials ... Metz falls to U.S. Third Army, except for pockets; the commander has been captured ...British Second Army threatens to turn the northern flank of the Westwall ... First and Ninth Armies are smashing slowly but steadily toward Cologne ... Germans may be abandoning Duren ... Berlin reports great new Soviet offensive in Latvia, where 400,000 Germans are pinned against the Baltic sea around Liepaja ... Reds encircle Miskolo in Hungary on three sides, and enter it from the south; the city is 80 miles northeast of Budapest ... In Albania port of Durazzo falls to Albanian partisans ... Omura and Nagasaki on Jan island of Kyushu are bombed by U.S. B-29s, in strength ... carrier-based planes attack Manila area, setting two ships afire and destroying 118 planes ... All U.S. Army air bases in southwestern China now are in Jap hands.

Nov. 24, 1944 - Large force of U.S. B-29s bombs Tokyo during night, the first raid on that capital since Doolittle hit it in April of 1942 ... Yokohama and Kobe also were believed bombed ... planes were based on Saipan in the Marianas ... 32nd Division has captured Limon on Leyte in the Philippines ... Soviets resume offensive in eastern Czechoslovakia west of Ungvar, gaining up to 16 miles along the 25-mile front ... Reds capture wine center of Tokaj in northern Hungary ... French Second Armored Division is driving toward Rhine city of Strasbourg ... in north Germans register slight gains against British Second Army ... U.S. Third and Seventh Armies are linked, and are driving toward the Saar.

Nov. 30, 1944 - Tokyo radio howls murder after third B-29 raid in six days, and threatens to kill all U.S. fliers falling upon Japan ... this last attack apparently was a heavy one ... Iwo Jima in the Volcano islands also was bombed ... Heavy rains again stall ground activity on Leyte in Philippines ... U.S. Ninth Army in Germany launches new drive in Geilenkirchen sector, 12 miles north of Aachen, hitting toward the Roer river area, Dusseldorf and Cologne ... the army is 27 miles southwest of Dusseldorf ... Third Army is driving into Saar basin on 50-mile front, one division being two miles west of Saarlautern ... Seventh Army north of Strasbourg is only 12 miles from Bavaria ... New Soviet offensive is fanning out across the plains of southern Hungary ... Pecs has been taken by storm and the advance continues on a 93-mile front below Budapest ... north of the capital the Reds break into Eger ... the new drive appears aimed to encircle Budapest, to cut off the Germans in the Balkans, or to invade Austria.

December 1944

A Reverent Hush

Music ushered in the last month of the year in Green Bay. Patrons at Hutson's Playdium listened to Patricia O'Dare on the huge Hammond organ. Ethel Nagel was at the piano at the Zuider Zee, while Stan Olsen entertained at the electric organ at the Hotel Northland. On the west side, the Zunker Rhythm Boys were a hit at the Silver Rail Bar.

That welcomed the adult population. But a teenager identified as B.H.J. had his letter printed in the *Green Bay Press-Gazette* in which he complained about the lack of recreational outlets for his generation.

"We are expected to go out into Green Bay factories and work just as hard and harder than lots of men, and at a much lower rate of pay," he wrote, "and we are still not supposed to have any recreation. Let's go, Green Bay. Keep teenagers out of the taverns and give us something to do at night."

The Green Bay Catholic Diocese gained a bishop as Grand Island, Nebraska, Bishop Stanislaus Bona was appointed by Pope Pius XII as coadjutor to Green Bay Bishop Paul Rhode, whose health was in decline.

Former Packer Francis (Jug) Earp was named acting director of the Green Bay Office of Price Administration after administering tire rationing for OPA.

John Byrnes arrived in Washington, D.C., to begin his first term as the Eighth District congressman. And a plane in the fleet of the Eighth Air Force in England was named "Miss Green Bay" by Master Sgt. Elmer Villiesse, a Green Bay native and plane mechanic.

The war's impact remained strong and visible.

Eighty-five high school senior boys aged seventeen and eighteen went to Milwaukee to take an exam for possible entry into a radar school for the US Navy. The need to replace men sent to the battlefront in Europe had grown.

The Brown County area was well represented at a postwar agriculture conference in Madison. And veterans who were discharged after serving at least ninety days or because of injury were beginning to take advantage of the new GI Bill of Rights to further their education.

The war contributed to a reduced total of inmates at the Wisconsin State Reformatory in Allouez, and officials said the education of those imprisoned was beginning to show positive results despite the fact that St. Norbert College was no longer able to send students there as practice teachers.

As the holidays neared, 200 students from the Green Bay high schools were excused from afternoon classes until the holiday break to help overworked store clerks.

***

The muddled Eastern Division pro football race wasn't cleared up the first weekend of the month. The Giants defeated the Redskins 16-13 at the Polo Grounds while Philadelphia beat Brooklyn. The Giants would be division champs if they could win in Washington the following weekend, but if they lost and the Eagles beat Cleveland, the Packers would be traveling to Philadelphia for the title game.

Lambeau took a train to New York to scout the Giants-Redskins

> ## Local News Highlights
>
> **December 4:** Rep. LaVern Dilweg, defeated in the November election by John Byrnes, said he is considering opening a branch law office in Washington, D.C.
>
> **December 12:** Approximately 300 deer hunters from six states hunting in Wisconsin have been reported to their local war price and rationing boards because they exceeded their gasoline rations.

game while former Packer Eddie Kotal went to Philadelphia to scout the Eagles. That left Hutson and assistant George Trafton to supervise the Packers' workouts in Green Bay.

At least that was the plan. But heavy snowfalls in Green Bay prompted the Packers to travel sooner to the University of Virginia in Charlottesville, where they would work out and await their next destination.

They didn't have to wait long. The Giants, with former Packer and Green Bay native Arnie Herber throwing three touchdown passes,

Don Hutson (left) leads the Packers in warmups following a major snowstorm in Green Bay prior to leaving for the East Coast and the championship game. (Green Bay Press-Gazette photo)

smothered the Redskins 31-0. The Packers would have a rematch with the Giants at the Polo Grounds.

With the date, location and opponent known, the pre-game chatter quickened.

National columnist Grantland Rice noted that the Packers were an early 5-9 favorite by one betting source.

"The always dangerous Packers will be much harder to handle than they were three weeks ago when they had the western title packed away on ice," Rice wrote.

Al Del Greco of the *Bergen Evening Record* in New York wrote:

Versatile Packers lineman Forrest McPherson was a ninth-year veteran out of the University of Nebraska during the 1944 season. (Green Bay Press-Gazette photo)

"By all signs, the Giants should beat the stuffings out of Green Bay ... but don't be too sure."

Giants head coach Steve Owen reacted to the early betting line. "I like it that way. Let 'em make the Packers a top-heavy favorite but, personally, I think it's an even game all the way."

Tommy Holmes of the *Brooklyn Eagle* was pulling for the Giants, but cautious.

"I hope that Stout Steve (Owen) caps his grand 1944 coaching job with a league championship. Still, it's hard to bet against Hutson. In the words of Dr. Jack Sutherland after watching the Ghost (Hutson) for the first time, 'A most remarkable young man. Sometimes he looks one way and runs another. But more surprising still, sometimes he looks one way and runs that way.'"

Two days before the game, Rice wrote about the conditions of the teams.

"While the Giants have been taking two hard batterings from the Washington Redskins, the Packers have been leading the life of Riley and the easy road.

"The Giants proved three weeks ago they could take the Packers apart. But at that time Lambeau knew he had the western championship in his grip, and so he was taking no chances with his team – especially his all-time star, the country boy, by the name of Don Hutson.

"Owen wrapped up Sammy Baugh nicely. A short while back Owen administered the same cobra poison to Hutson. The Giants, in shape, proved a short while back they were a better team than Lambeau's western invaders. They still have the better all-around strength."

And Owen, two days before the title game, said: "The fact that we stopped the Packers a month ago doesn't mean we are going to do it again. The Packers will come here with three weeks rest and the title will be at stake. Every man will be fighting for the winners' share. We figure on seeing a lot more of Hutson, Comp and Fritsch than we did last time. Green Bay will be a lot harder to beat."

The relationship between Lambeau and Giants assistant coach Red Smith surfaced the week before the game when United Press reporter

Jack Cuddy approached Smith on the Giants' practice field.

"I do not choose to comment upon my previous relations with Lambeau," Smith told Cuddy. "I cannot recall having any difficulties with him or with the Packer club. I will break down and confess, however, that I hope we beat hell outta them Sunday."

In his published article, Cuddy wrote that "from Midwestern sportswriters we learn that Curly Lambeau, Packer coach, attributes a portion of his outfit's success this season to the fact that Red Smith is no longer their mentor."

Noting Smith's upbringing in Combined Locks just south of Green Bay, Cuddy wrote: "The Smiths of Kaukauna will be chortling if Sportscaster Harry Wismer's machine-gun account of the game over the Blu network details an impressive Giant victory. The pride and prowess of the Smiths will have been upheld to the discomfiture of Monsieur Lambeau."

National sportswriter Bob Considine added a little pre-game drama: "There is another side to Sunday's game: a revenge angle. Arnie Herber, the old Packer passer Owen revived this season. Seems he and his veteran Packer owner-coach Curly Lambeau parted on speaking terms after the 1941 season – but the words they were speaking weren't printable."

Considine didn't elaborate.

The only drama for the Packers occurred two days before the game when they learned that their scheduled train from Charlottesville to New York was four hours late. After a morning light workout at the New Armory, Lambeau rushed his team to the C&O train depot to catch an earlier train.

"This is serious," he told a reporter. "We've got to get to New York sometime. This is the biggest thing in their lives and they are in perfect condition thanks to the ideal weather here while we were practicing."

The Packers were listed as 2-1 and 8-5 favorites, and several writers were puzzled by it.

"Although they were kicked all over the Polo Grounds four weeks

Paul Duhart was a rookie back out of the University of Florida during the Packers' 1944 championship season. (Green Bay Press-Gazette photo)

ago ... the Green Bay Packers will be the favorite when they collide with the Manhattan Monsters," wrote Raymond Johnson of the *Nashville Tennessean*. "The reason the wise guys think the Wisconsin veterans will take their sixth world title is that they have had three weeks rest."

Others leaned toward a Giants victory.

"I wouldn't be too sure about the Packers winning," wrote Bill Lee of the *Hartford Courant*. "Paschal or no Paschal, the Giants still have Steve Owen."

And Billy Kelly of the *Buffalo Courier Express* took exception with the odds that favored the Packers.

"We think he (the oddsmaker) has the favorite and the odds reversed," he wrote. "We lean to the Giants."

But there was general pessimism in New York in the days leading up to the game. One reason was the condition of Giants star running back Bill Paschal, who sprained his ankle against the Redskins.

"It has slowed me down," Paschal said two days before the game. "Just tape it up and let me loose."

The other damper for the Giants was the weather.

Dick Young of the *New York Daily News* wrote that a frozen Polo Grounds field would hurt the Giants' running attack and hamper its defensive linemen trying to get to Packers quarterback Irv Comp.

"Degree by degree, as the mercury is driven down by New York wintry winds, the Giants' victory chances ... drop correspondingly," Young wrote.

Giants president Jack Mara said, "This hard ground is bad for us."

Mrs. William Boncher leads a team in wrapping Christmas boxes to send overseas for local military members, December 13, 1944. (Green Bay Press-Gazette photo)

Then something more important happened in the world the day before the game.

***

It was known officially as the Ardennes Offensive, but history tagged it the Battle of the Bulge. A strong German counteroffensive in the dense forest between Belgium and Luxembourg pushed the US First and Third armies back on their heels and became the bloodiest US battle of the war. It would be ten days before the US troops around Bastogne, Belgium, would be rescued and the German gains halted and reversed.

The *Press-Gazette* went to press before reports of the German offensive reached the newsroom that Saturday. The newspaper set aside front page space to inform readers that its future Saturday editions would be reduced to fourteen pages in an effort to meet the newsprint limitations required by the War Production Board.

The Monday, December 18, edition carried the banner headline "Americans Battle to Stem Great German Counterattack."

Two days later, responding to news reports that indicated the Germans may have benefitted by information provided by Belgian informants who told where the weaker Allied defenses were located, the *Press-Gazette* used its editorial page to react.

"Numerous Belgian informants aided the Germans in getting this information. There can be no doubt about that fact. It should be evident that unless Eisenhower can control with a rigid hand the territory back of him, restrict all traffic through it, compel citizens to carry permits to move, and send out of the district or place in concentration camps dissident or suspicious elements, then his army is weakened if not imperiled by the situation."

The siege would continue until the day after Christmas when US forces, finally aided by clear skies that allowed its air power to drive the Germans back, would signal the end to the Bulge.

As the country was absorbing news of the Bulge that third week of the month, it was also informed that the US Supreme Court ruled that citizens of Japanese descent, who were forced out of their West Coast homes early in the war and housed in settlement camps, were permitted to return to their homes.

***

The German surge, which included the temporary encirclement of US forces in Bastogne, came at a time when voices were being raised about the continuation of competitive sports when wartime manpower needs were high.

James Byrnes, War Mobilization Director, sent a directive to Selective Services Director General Lewis B. Hershey to have him re-examine all professional athletes who have been deferred or discharged from military service for physical reasons.

Byrnes said it was "difficult for the public to understand" how a large number of men between the ages of eighteen and twenty-six could be unfit for military service and yet be able to compete with the "greatest athletes of the nation. In the cases of those rejected for punctured ear drums, for instance, they seem to hear the signals all right. I imagine that they could hear the first sergeant all right.

"And for those tricky knees that seem to stand up on the ball field all right, I suppose they would be able to stand up at, say, Verdun."

Red Grange, president of a newly forming U.S. Football League, said, "If conditions in this war continue as they are right now, I don't think any league should operate. We don't want to operate without a go-ahead from Washington. We'll just sit tight and wait."

But NFL commissioner Elmer Layden, after pointing out that his league has fulfilled every wartime governmental requirement and would continue to do so, said sports served as an instrument of relaxation and recreation for both civilian and military sports fans.

"I feel competitive athletics inspire the youth of America to embrace the qualities of loyalty and teamwork, the two fundamentals of patriotism," he said.

"We just want to wait and see what happens," Layden said. "I don't think there is a player in the league who wouldn't be in service if they'd take him. We have a number of 4-Fs and some medical discharges. We want to win the war first and play football second. If we have enough players, we'll probably play. If not, we'll wait until we have them."

Lambeau weighed in by saying Byrnes's effort would have little impact on the Packers "unless there is a drastic lowering of physical standards for military service."

Byrnes did order all horse and dog tracks to cease operations by January 3, 1945.

Left unresolved at year's end was the status of potential rival pro football leagues.

United Press reporter Jack Cuddy was in New York for the owners meeting the day after the championship game and approached an unnamed owner. He told the man that pro football must be reaping a rich harvest since outsiders are trying to muscle in on the gravy.

"Sonny, you – and a lot of other misguided folks – are laboring under a delusion," he told Cuddy. "Only five clubs in the National league did well enough financially to break even during the 1944 season. They were Green Bay, the Chicago Bears, New York, Washington and Philadelphia. All the rest lost money. They wound up in the red at a time when there's more money in circulation than ever before in the country's history."

George Barton of the *Minneapolis Morning Tribune* wrote that the NFL owners have themselves to blame if the competition got hot.

"The niggardly salaries paid by owners ... even the Chicago Bears owned by George Halas, and the Green Bay Packers owned by a group of Green Bay businessmen headed by Curly Lambeau, plus the high-handed methods employed by the sponsors are chiefly responsible for opposition loops entering the field. The new leagues are backed by wealthy men who are determined to make their circuits successful."

As the populace looked back at the eventful 1944, it held the hope that 1945 would bring the conclusion of the war, the generational event that was certain to play a major role in everyone's future.

Before Christmas, the *Press-Gazette* printed an editorial steeped in a form of prayer.

"On Christmas Eve a great and reverent hush will creep around the world despite the wrathful sounds of rattling machine guns and belching cannon. It will be the spontaneous silence that comes to men everywhere, and with a bewildered rush to the youth in mind and perilous misery as they try to reconcile the godly message of 'peace on earth' with what they see before them."

***

(The following war updates were provided by Major John M. Walter in his role as the orientation and communications officer at Camp Wolters in Mineral Wells, Texas. He wrote the daily war updates for the base and included them in his personal diary.)

Dec. 1, 1944 - Seventy percent of German war industry in Ruhr, Saar and Rhône are menaced by advancing Allied armies ... Ninth Army now holds 10-mile stretch of Roer river northeast of Aachen ... Ninth is crowding Linnich and Julich on the road to Dusseldorf and Cologne ... First Army is preparing to storm Duren, 20 miles southwest of the advance ... Third Army, closing in on Merzig, engages in heavy artillery duel along Saar ... German artillery hits Strasbourg, now occupied by the U.S. Seventh Army ... The seventh attempt of the Japanese to reinforce their Leyte garrison ends in disaster, as U.S. planes sink four transports off Ormic with loss of 5,000 Japs ... Heavy rains on Leyte keep ground forces bottled up ... Two Soviet armies are driving across the Hungarian plain ... one was pushing across fallen Pecs to a point 100 miles from Austria ... Eger and Szikszo are occupied north of Budapest.

Dec. 4, 1944 - Chinese leaders believe nation's fate may be decided in next two months ... Japs are 50 miles from Kweiyang, capital of Kweichow province ... Fourth raid by B-29s on Tokyo was toughest

Crowds gather in downtown Green Bay to celebrate the end of the war against Japan (V-J Day), August 14, 1945. Victory in Europe Day (V-E Day) occurred May 8, 1945. (Green Bay Press-Gazette photo)

and most successful to date ... Leyte island action continues at standstill due to tropical rains ... Third Army troops are pouring across Saar river and into Saarlautern ... Ninth Army troops fight into Linnich and Julich along Roer river line ... British Second Army steps off at dawn and breaks into streets of Venlo on Holland-German border ... Advance Cossack units are fighting Germans along east shore of Lake Balaton in Hungray, with the main Soviet forces 21 miles away at Tamasi ... Heavy fighting continues around Faenz in Italy.

Dec. 7, 1944 - The United States has been at war three years today ... I suspect we are closer to the end than the beginning, although the business against the Japs may take longer than we think ... United States B-29s observe the infamous day by bombing Mukden in Manchuria, and Tokyo ... Clearing weather on Leyte stirs up ground operations ... On the Chinese mainland the city of Tuhshan, 75 miles southeast of Kweiyang in Kweichow province, falls to the Japs ... Soviets are 35 miles from the Austrian frontier, and have launched a new assault upon Budapest ... Only activity on Western front consists of slow but steady advances by Third Army, which is three and a half miles from Saarbrucken.

Dec. 9, 1944 - Stockholm reports say Germans are building huge rocket installations in Norwegian mountains, presumably for aiming the robots at the United States east coast ... U.S. Third Army troops continue to pour into German Saar across four new bridgeheads over the Saar river ... Germans counterattack heavily north of Saarlautern, but the assault is repelled and the Americans capture 12 pillboxes ... Berlin reports American First and Ninth Armies regrouping for new offensive against Cologne ... Soviet armies are rolling up to Budapest on two sides, and savage tank battles rage on the approaches to the city ... moving west from captured Hatvan, the Soviets take Vac, 15 miles northeast of the capital, and another column is 13 miles out in the south ... Chinese forces in Kweichow province deal the Japs a smashing defeat, driving them back 20 to 30 miles after the advance had reached to within 75 miles of Kweiyang ... On Leyte, the 77th Division advances three miles to take Camp Downs on the outskirts of Ormoc ... Heavy task force attack is made on Iwo Jima in the Volcano group ... Japs say B-29s were over the inland sea between Honshu and Kyushu.

Dec. 13, 1944 - Germans apparently plan defense west of Rhine river, as no withdrawal is indicated ... four United States armies are poised along an All-American front ... First Army now holds 10 miles of Roer's west bank, and is 1,000 yards from Duren ... Seventh Army races 16 miles toward Karlsruhe, and is within 15 miles of that city, capital of Baden ... Hard fighting rages on approaches to Budapest ... Meeting of Roosevelt, Stalin, Churchill is planned for late January ... Greek civil war continues unabated ... Large force of B-29s attacks Nagoya, third largest Jap city ... Bonin and Volcano islands are taking almost daily poundings ... Dwindling Cap garrison on Leyte is denied reinforcements, as American planes break up new convoy, sinking five transports and four destroyers ... Chinese have punched 20 miles into Kwangsi province, exploiting their counteroffensive.

Dec. 18, 1944 - Powerful German counteroffensive against U.S. First and Ninth Army sectors hurls Americans back from German soil and nullifies the danger to Cologne ... front is fluid along 70-mile stretch and Malmedy in Belgium is menaced ... Seventh Army takes three more towns in Wissembourg gap opposite Bavaria ... Soviet armory crashes into town five and a half miles northeast of Budapest ... Powerful new blows by American Superforts are struck at Japan from east and west ... more than 100 of the sky giants bomb Nagoya on Honshu island, and another fleet hits Hankow in Hopeh province of China ... U.S. forces on Mindanao gain another mile during night ... 25,000 Japs left on Leyte are split into three parts, and the 77th and 32nd Divisions are only six miles apart ... Chinese troops are one mile from Hochih in Kweichow province.

Dec. 21, 1944 - Fourteen or 15 German divisions are swarming into the Belgian breach in the First Army's lines ... bad weather has grounded Allied planes ... the situation is expected to get worse before it gets better ... Soviet troops are only 17 miles from Losing in southern Czechoslovakia ... The Yamashita line on Leyte has been smashed and the Japs are retreating to the north ... the fight for Ormoc corridor is over ... Bitter fighting is reported south of Bologna in Italy.

Dec. 24, 1944 - German troops are rolling toward Meuse river in Belgium, being within 14 miles of the river on a 13-mile front ... First and Third armies are hammering away at the flanks ... Bastogne is encircled, but the Americans therein have scorned surrender ... Reds have cut last escape route westward from Budapest and are within 10 miles of completely surrounding the capital ... they are less than 100 miles from Vienna ... MacArthur declares the campaigns for Leyte and Samar in the Philippines are finished, with the Japs suffering the worst defeat in their history ... Churchill and Eden are in Athens, attempting to help smooth out the Greek civil war.

Dec. 28, 1944 - In a tremendous counteroffensive, Allied forces in Belgium have narrowed the neck of the German salient to 20 miles ... they have regained the initiative for the first time since the Germans attacked 16 December ... the besieged garrison at Bastogne has been relieved ... the Allies are striking violently on the flanks ... Soviets have crossed the Danube river north of Budapest to split the city ... two Red columns are 96 miles from Vienna ... Japs beaten back in futile attack on Mindoro.

Dec. 30, 1944 - Westernmost thrust of the German army has been driven back 12 miles by the First Army, to the edge of Rochefort, the Nazis now are 15 miles from the Meuse ... Patton has widened the corridor to Bastogne ... good weather has returned to the western front, and Allied bombers and fighters are everywhere ... Soviets break into new sections of Budapest, where the fighting is similar to that in Stalingrad ...the Reds farther north are 90 miles from Vienna ... Japs still insist large convoy is on move around Mindoro in the Philippines ... MacArthur has ordered internment of all Filipinos who aided Japs at any time ... Two new British fleets are joining the American Navy in the Pacific.

***

The Championship Game
December 17, 1944

It would be hard to find another game of championship proportions that was impacted as heavily by the opening coin flip.

The Giants won the toss, but rather than choosing to receive the kickoff, they decided to take the end of the Polo Grounds field that would give them the wind at their back. It came with the assumption that the Packers would then choose to receive.

But offensive football in 1944 wasn't known for explosive plays, and Lambeau would say later that Owen outsmarted himself by choosing the wind.

"We gambled on winning the toss and kicking off to the Giants so as to put them in the hole right at the start, and we worked on kickoffs for ten days before the game," Lambeau said. "Steve (Owen) appeared to work on the old theory that all the Packers and Bears want is to get their hands on the ball. Well, he won the toss and Don Hutson was discouraged, believing they would choose to kick. Don almost fell over when the Giant captain chose the goal with the wind at his back, thinking that we would naturally choose to receive. Well, we didn't. We kicked and had them right back in their own territory throughout the first half."

Former Packers passer and Green Bay native Arnie Herber came out of retirement to play for the New York Giants in the 1944 and 1945 seasons. (Green Bay Press-Gazette photo)

The Giants would go without a single first down in the first half. They punted five times in the first period alone, once on third down, and Joe Laws intercepted Herber on another series.

The Packers also benefitted by Owen's habit of regularly substituting players because it led to ten delay of game penalties. He had hoped to substitute when the clock stopped on an incomplete pass, but the Packers only attempted eleven passes in the game.

"We either had a first down with five yards to go or they had a first down with 15 yards to go," Lambeau said. "I think if we had opened up with our passing, we might have run up a higher score. Under Steve's two-team backfield system, where he changes units on offense and defense, he had to make most of his substitutions on his own three timeouts per half."

The first period was a series of punts by both teams, with the Packers managing to reach the Giants' 34-yard line after Irv Comp completed a pass to Hutson. But the drive ended when Comp was intercepted.

The second period was decisive for the Packers as they started at the Giants' 48-yard line after Comp's 21-yard punt return. On the first play of the period, Joe Laws cut behind a perfect trap block from Larry Craig and ran for twenty yards. Ted Fritsch broke through the line on the next play and ran all the way to the 1-yard line before being tackled.

Two more Fritsch carries and one by Laws gained nothing, and the Packers called a timeout. The play then went to Fritsch, who bulled into the end zone over right tackle on fourth down. Hutson kicked the extra point.

After an exchange of punts and another Laws interception of a Herber pass, the Packers drove for a decisive score. It was set up by a Comp-to-Hutson pass that carried to the New York 30. On the next play, Hutson lined up on the right, broke downfield and cut to his right, taking three Giants defenders with him.

Fritsch broke into the left flat and was all alone to take a Comp pass at the 10-yard line, and ran untouched into the end zone.

Giants right defensive end Frank Liebel was supposed to drop back and cover the area where Fritsch caught the pass, but he was lured over to Hutson's side. Both Mel Hein and Howie Livingston tried to recover and ran toward Fritsch, but it was too late.

Giants assistant coach Red Smith shook his head when asked about the play after the game.

"You know, we practiced that play at least twenty-five times this week, and never once could we make it work against those same players who were fooled today," Smith said.

Owen said, "That was a ridiculous thing."

Said Hutson: "Golly, I thought I had the whole Giant team on my tail. I was running so fast that I didn't stop to count 'em, but I felt as the play was happening that it was going to work."

Joe Trimble, covering the game for the *New York Daily News*, wrote: "It is hard to believe but the play that beat the Giants at the Polo Grounds was an antique which has been in the Green Bay repertoire for years and one which the Giants practiced against all week."

The Packers took their 14-0 lead into halftime. The intermission entertainment was a group of tumblers from Ringling Bros. and Barnum & Bailey Circus.

Giants owner Jack Mara was walking to the Giants locker room when a fan hollered, "Hey, Mara. You've given us a circus. Now how about a first down?"

The Giants received the second-half kickoff and on their first play from scrimmage, Bill Paschal, who was the leading rusher in the league, tried to go up the middle. His injured ankle gave out and he was helped off the field and didn't return. Ward Cuff was left to do most of the ball carrying.

Another interception by Laws ended one New York drive, but on the last play of the third period, Herber completed a long pass to Frank Liebel. Comp was covering him, but fell and Liebel was finally pushed out of bounds by Fritsch at the 1-yard line. Cuff scored the touchdown on the first play of the final quarter.

The Giants would make one more drive into Packers territory, but Paul Duhart intercepted Herber at the Green Bay 20. The Giants would get the ball once more at their own 34, but a fourth-down pass to Cuff came up short and the game ended with the Packers winning, 14-7.

The Packers divvied up the $41,836 winner's share of the Polo Grounds gate receipts while the Giants got $27,938. It meant that the Packers each received $1,478.68, while each Giant got $830.78. The

Packers voted to split their playoff pool into twenty-seven full shares, five half-shares and one quarter share.

Lambeau gave the game ball to Baby Ray, who lived in Nashville.

"We let him down badly in his home town by losing a preseason exhibition game against the Eagles, and we promised him then and there that he'd get the ball when we won the world's championship."

Reactions to the Packers' victory came from all over.

Grantland Rice, syndicated national columnist: "Green Bay, a pleasant Wisconsin hamlet of some 50,000 souls, took charge of New York's 7,000,000 city slickers. To have the smaller hamlets from the Midwest rub it in even harder on the Giant metropolis, Ted Fritsch of the Stevens Point Teachers College took over the show."

Jack Miller, *Troy* (Ohio) *Daily News*: "We were glad to see the Green Bay Packers win. One reason is that in some dispatches from syndicated sportswriters in the east, some jibes were made at Curly Lambeau. It was hinted that Curly was not an outstanding coach. It was baldly stated that one thing that favored the Giants was the team had much better coaching."

Billy Kelly, *Buffalo Courier Express*: "Well, the boys who lay the odds and figure the points picked the right team."

Paul Menton, *Baltimore Evening Sun*: "Green Bay assumes the position it seemed destined for since early season when it loomed as the best team among the war torn squads of the National League."

Tommy Holmes, *Brooklyn Eagle*: "After all, the Packers did enter the playoff with three full weeks of rest, a tremendous boon to the many veteran players in the Green Bay lineup."

Joe Williams, *Rome* (New York) *Daily Sentinel*: "Indeed, I think it is a mild indictment against the Packers that they didn't win more emphatically."

Frank Cope, Giants captain: "I think if we were to play the Packers again next week, and we had Paschal and all hands ready and the Packers hadn't had three weeks rest, we would win just as we did before the playoff. But that's not what they pay for."

Patterson, New Jersey, sportswriter Harry Levenstein, on the fact that the Giants had to keep playing in December while the Packers were idle: "There should be some sort of law against a set-up of that kind with the limited number of players that the clubs have access to."

Harvey Boyle of the *Pittsburgh Post-Gazette* wrote that NFL owners needed to follow baseball's system in scheduling.

"The National Football League moguls could well spend the winter figuring out how to reform a schedule-making which is sadly in need of same," he wrote. "The league ought to give every team in the league the same number of home dates and dates away from home. The season, as in baseball, ought to have a common date for ending. We trust we won't have to speak of these grave matters again. To work, men, and at once."

Hutson's pass receiving domination was evident in the NFL's season statistics. He scored 85 points (second was 66), caught 58 passes (second was 39) for 866 yards (second was 505). Football historians will note that defensive backs weren't as fast during that NFL era, further emphasizing the impact that Hutson had on future defenses that had to be built to stop such talented receivers.

A topic of conversation and speculation immediately after the game was Hutson's future as a player. Speaking to reporters, Hutson said he was finished as a player.

"I'll never play another game in New York or anywhere else," he said. "I have a coaching contract with Lambeau and I'm just going to coach."

Lambeau, who has heard Hutson's retirement claims in the past, said, "Oh, he feels that way at the end of every season. He'll play again."

Teammate Buckets Goldenberg chimed in, "What's that you said? Your fourth annual retirement?"

"Right," Hutson replied. "If I ever play another game in New York, I'll jump off the Empire State Building."

Giants coach Steve Owen entered the Packers locker room after the game and heard Hutson's comment. He asked Hutson to put his statement in writing and sign it.

"I will give you an affidavit later," Hutson said.

"He means 1947," Owen said with a smile.

Two days later, Hutson softened his retirement pledge.

"If the Packers can get new material or get former players discharged from the service to help defend the title, I won't play next fall," he said. "If they need me, I probably will play."

Hutson's role in the pro football offensive evolution was borne out in the league's pass receiving statistics. He caught 488 passes in his career for 7,991 yards and 99 touchdowns. His touchdown record stood for over forty years and the game he helped change eventually produced twelve receivers who have surpassed Hutson's 99. One of them is former Packer Davante Adams.

Despite his repeated vows to retire as a player, Hutson would play one more season and score ten more touchdowns. When the first Pro Football Hall of Fame class was announced in 1963, Hutson was a shoo-in.

Dante Lavelli, who had a standout career as a pass receiver for the Cleveland Browns, presented Hutson at his HOF induction.

"Each bright new receiver is hailed as a second Don Hutson and later perhaps as a better than Hutson," Lavelli said. "Then time turns the page on that player and Don is left to wait the next comparison to come up. Hutson created pass patterns and developed faking to an almost federal offense."

Eddie Jones of the *Minneapolis Times* wrote, "New York writers report that Curly Lambeau may retire next season to the front office and make Don Hutson head coach of the Green Bay Packers."

The 1945 season became Hutson's final one as a player, while Lambeau would coach the team for five more years.

The Packers were welcomed home at 10:20 pm on a Monday after a twenty-four-hour train trip from New York. An estimated 1,500 fans braved the 5-degree temperatures and gathered at the Milwaukee Road depot. Sirens blared and the Lumberjack Band played as the team stepped off the train.

Lambeau and assistant George Trafton had stayed in New York

Packers fans flocked to the Milwaukee Road depot to welcome the team back to Green Bay, December 18, 1944. This tradition continues today as fans gather at Austin Straubel International Airport to welcome the team home after games. (Green Bay Press-Gazette photo)

for the league meeting earlier that day, and a couple of players went directly from New York to their homes.

Pete Tinsley had arrived earlier in the day after learning that his wife had given birth to their son that morning at St. Mary's Hospital.

Packers president Lee Joannes said that since part of the team was already scattered, a victory banquet would probably be planned for August.

A ten-minute film of the championship game was shown at the Bay Theater for the final week of the year. It was part of the Bay's regular program that included the latest Gary Cooper film *Casanova Brown*. The *Press-Gazette* ad read, "Don Hutson knows his passes but so does Casanova Brown."

How good were the 1944 Packers? As the dust settled around the team's championship accomplishment, some attempted to give it context.

Tommy Timlin, who refereed the Army-Navy football game in Baltimore two weeks before the NFL playoff and then attended the Packers-Giants game, left no doubt about which football team he thought was the best in the country.

"The best team in the country was Army," Timlin told reporters. "No question about it. They'd beat Green Bay by four touchdowns."

National columnist Grantland Rice poured his praise on Army's backfield tandem of Glenn Davis and Doc Blanchard.

"I know the Giants, Packers, Eagles and Redskins had no backfield that was even close to Army's," he wrote.

Most of the newspaper headlines throughout the country included Ted Fritsch's name, since he scored both Packers touchdowns. But if they had voted for a most valuable player in the championship game of 1944, common sense would have put Joe Laws's name up front. His three interceptions alone made the difference, but he was also the leading ground-gainer with 74 yards.

The 1944 championship was in the books, but the wartime season would be the last time the Packers even flirted with the title until Lt. John Kennedy became President Kennedy, war hero Dwight Eisenhower completed two terms as president, and City Stadium (later Lambeau Field) replaced farm fields off Highland Avenue (later Lombardi Avenue) west of the Fox River.

The three seasons after 1944 showed winning records – barely – but then the free fall began. By 1949, only five of the thirty-one players from the 1944 championship team were still with the team. There began the series of head coaching changes, and failures, until a fix was found.

Lombardi.

Player Biographies

Paul Berezney
Born: September 25, 1915
City: Jersey City, New Jersey
College: Fordham
Size: 6-2, 220 - Right tackle
Military: Army veteran of Korean War, volunteer surgeon for Vietnam War
Packers: 1942-1945
After football: 1943 graduate of Marquette University Medical School; thoracic surgeon in St. Petersburg, Florida, retired in 1970
Died: March 29, 1990
City: Toms River, New Jersey

Dick Bilda
Born: May 17, 1919
City: Milwaukee, Wisconsin
College: Marquette
Size: 6-2, 210 - Back
Packers: Played one season for the Packers and got into three games
After football: Member of Marquette University High School Hall of Fame
Died: November 29, 1996
City: Milwaukee, Wisconsin

Charley Brock
Born: March 15, 1916
City: Columbus, Nebraska
College: Nebraska
Size: 6-2, 207 - Center
Packers: Played nine seasons, 1939-47
After football: Coached for Packers in 1949; Packers Hall of Fame in 1973; employed by philanthropist Victor McCormick and sold insurance for 15 years; very active in Packers Alumni organization; second cousin to teammate Lou Brock
Died: May 25, 1987
City: Green Bay, Wisconsin

Lou Brock
Born: December 9, 1917
City: Stafford, Kansas
College: Purdue
Size: 6-0, 195 - Halfback
Packers: Played 1940-45
After football: Packers Hall of Fame in 1982; worked in real estate and operated family farm near Stafford; second cousin to teammate Charley Brock
Died: May 5, 1989
City: Stafford, Kansas

Mike Bucchianeri
Born: January 9, 1917
City: Van Voorhis, Pennsylvania
College: Indiana
Size: 5-10, 212 - Guard
Packers: 1941, 1944-45
After football: Coached at St. Norbert College; worked as a high school referee; was offensive line coach at Marquette University; implement sales manager for Green Bay Drop Forge
Died: February 19, 1992
City: Ocala, Florida

Tony Canadeo
Born: May 5, 1919
City: Chicago, Illinois
College: Gonzaga
Size: 5-11, 190 - Halfback, tailback, fullback
Military: Served in US Army
Packers: 1941-52. Played in three games in 1944 and none in 1945 due to military service.
After football: Steel salesman; Packers radio play-by-play announcer with Ray Scott; Packers Hall of Fame 1973; Pro Football Hall of Fame 1974; Packers executive committee member; his No. 3 was retired by the Packers in 1952.
Died: November 29, 2003
City: Green Bay, Wisconsin

Irv Comp

Born: May 17, 1919
City: Milwaukee, Wisconsin
College: Benedictine
Size: 6-2, 204 - Tailback
Military: Ineligible because he was blind in one eye
Packers: 1943-49; intercepted 10 passes in 1943, a Packers record
After football: Packers Hall of Fame in 1986; worked for Miller Brewing Company
Died: July 11, 1989
City: Woodruff, Wisconsin

Larry Craig

Born: June 27, 1916
City: Six Mile, South Carolina
College: South Carolina
Size: 6-1, 211 - Blocking back
Packers: 1939-49; played 121 straight games.
After football: Packers Hall of Fame in 1973; owned and operated a cattle farm in South Carolina
Died: May 30, 1992
City: Ninety Six, South Carolina

Milburn (Tiny) Croft

Born: November 7, 1920
City: Chicago, Illinois
College: Alabama, Ripon
Size: 6-3, 287 - Left tackle
Packers: 1942-47
After football: Manager for American Motors
Died: January 22, 1977
City: Woodruff, Wisconsin

Paul Duhart

Born: November 30, 1920
City: Montreal, Quebec (Canada)
College: Florida
Size: 6-0, 180 - Back
Military: Served in the army, discharged in 1944
Packers: 1944, then entered the 1945 draft and was chosen second overall by the Pittsburgh Steelers
After football: Successful high school teacher, football and golf coach in California; became a published poet.
Died: January 18, 2006
City: Huntington Beach, California

Bob Flowers

Born: August 6, 1917
City: Big Spring, Texas
College: Texas, Texas Tech
Size: 6-1, 201 - Center/Linebacker
Packers: 1942-49
After football: Sold cars; worked in farming and ranching business
Died: December 8, 1962, accidental shooting
City: Big Spring, Texas

Ted Fritsch

Born: October 31, 1920
City: Spencer, Wisconsin
College: Central State Teachers College, Stevens Point (Wisconsin)
Size: 5-10, 210 - Fullback
Military: Rejected, perforated eardrum
Packers: 1942-50
After football: Coached football at Central Catholic High School in Green Bay, renamed Premontre High School (now called Notre Dame de la Baie Academy, the school's football field is named Ted Fritsch Field); coached at St. Norbert College; worked for Green Bay Parks Department
Died: October 4, 1979
City: Green Bay, Wisconsin

War Year Champions

Charles (Buckets) Goldenberg
Born: April 15, 1911
City: Odessa, Russia
College: Wisconsin
Size: 5-10, 215 - Guard, Blocking back
Packers: 1933-45
After football: On the Packers Board of Directors 1953-85; owned Pappy's restaurant in Milwaukee; inducted into Packers Hall of Fame in 1971
Died: April 16, 1986
City: Glendale, Wisconsin

Don Hutson
Born: January 31, 1913
City: Pine Bluff, Arkansas
College: Alabama
Size: 6-1, 183 – Left end
Packers: 1935-45
After football: Assistant coach for the Packers; operated Packer Playdium bowling alley in Green Bay and Hutson Motors in Racine; charter member of Pro Football Hall of Fame in 1963; Packers Hall of Fame in 1972; the Packers' practice facility is named The Don Hutson Center
Died: June 26, 1997
City: Rancho Mirage, California

Harry Jacunski

Born: October 20, 1915
City: New Britain, Connecticut
College: Fordham (teammates with Vince Lombardi)
Size: 6-2, 200 – Right end
Military: Rejected by Navy in 1942
Packers: 1939-44
After football: Coached football at Notre Dame and Harvard, then 33 years at Yale
Died: February 20, 2003
City: Wallingford, Connecticut

Bob Kahler

Born: February 13, 1917
City: Grand Island, Nebraska
College: Nebraska
Size: 6-3, 201 – Defensive back, halfback
Military: Served in Air Force
Packers: 1942-44
After football: Coached college and high school football in Nebraska
Died: April 16, 2013
City: Palm Harbor, Florida

Bob Kercher

Born: January 14, 1919
City: German Township, Indiana
College: Georgetown
Size: 6-2, 196 - End
Packers: 1944
After football: Worked in oilfield supply business; became a golf pro
Died: January 4, 2004
City: Russell, Kansas

Bill Kuusisto

Born: April 26, 1918
City: Herman, Michigan
College: Minnesota
Size: 6-0, 228 - Guard
Packers: 1941-46
After football: Professional wrestler and referee
Died: May 28, 1973
City: Paynesville, Minnesota

Joe Laws

Born: June 16, 1911
City: Colfax, Iowa
College: Iowa
Size: 5-9, 186 - Halfback
Packers: 1934-45
After football: Packers Hall of Fame 1972; worked for Green Bay Poster Advertising
Died: August 22, 1979
City: Green Bay, Wisconsin

Joel Mason

Born: March 12, 1912
City: Iron River, Michigan
College: Western Michigan
Size: 6-0, 199 - End
Packers: 1942-45
After football: Assistant football coach at Wayne State, then head basketball coach there for 18 years
Died: October 31, 1995
City: Harper Woods, Michigan

Roy McKay

Born: February 2, 1920
City: Mason County, Texas
College: Texas
Size: 6-0, 193 – Tailback, halfback, fullback
Military: Served in Air Force
Packers: 1944-47
After football: Worked in auto sales; was an assistant high school football coach in Texas
Died: May 29, 1969
City: Sutton County, Texas

Forrest McPherson

Born: October 22, 1911
City: Fairbury, Nebraska
College: Nebraska
Size: 5-11, 233 – Guard, center, tackle
Packers: 1943-45; played two seasons with the Eagles and part of one season with the Bears in 1935
Died: October 7, 1989
City: Centralia, Washington

Tony Walter

(Photo courtesy UW-Platteville)

Don Perkins
Born: September 18, 1917
City: Dodgeville, Wisconsin
College: Wisconsin-Platteville
Size: 6-0, 196 - Back
Packers: 1943-45
After football: Lived in Waukegan, Illinois; drove truck for Leicht Transfer and Storage in Green Bay during the offseason.
Died: September 15, 1998
City: Branson, Missouri

Buford (Baby) Ray
Born: September 30, 1914
City: Una, Tennessee
College: Vanderbilt
Size: 6-6, 249 - Tackle
Packers: 1938-48
After football: Vanderbilt football recruiter and physical education director; Packers scout
Died: January 21, 1986
City: Nashville, Tennessee

Ade Schwammel

Born: October 14, 1908
City: Los Angeles, California
College: Oregon State
Size: 6-2, 225 - Tackle
Packers: 1934-36, 43-44
After football: In the clothing business; Tupperware distributor for Hawaii
Died: November 18, 1979
City: Honolulu, Hawaii

Glen Sorenson

Born: February 29, 1920
City: Salt Lake City, Utah
College: Utah State
Size: 6-0, 217 – Left guard
Packers: 1943-45
After football: Owned Lefty's Lounge in South Salt Lake, Utah
Died: February 26, 1972
City: Salt Lake City, Utah

Ben Starret
Born: November 19, 1917
City: Santa Rosa, California
College: St. Mary's (California)
Size: 5-11, 213; Blocking back, tailback
Packers: 1942-45; also played for Pittsburgh
Died: January 10, 1982
City: Burnt Ranch, California

Pete Tinsley
Born: March 16, 1913
City: Sumter, South Carolina
College: Georgia
Size: 5-8, 205; Right guard
Packers: 1938-45
After football: Coached football at Florence (Wis.) High School; Packers Hall of Fame 1979
Died: May 11, 1995
City: Iron Mountain, Michigan

Chuck Tollefson
Born: February 28, 1917
City: Elk Point, South Dakota
College: Iowa
Military: US Marine Corps
Size: 6-0, 215; Guard
Packers: 1944-46
After football: Sued Packers on a back pay issue and won a Wisconsin Supreme Court decision
Died: August 20, 1989
City: Green Bay, Wisconsin

Alex Urban
Born: July 16, 1917
City: Bessemer, Pennsylvania
College: South Carolina
Size: 6-3, 207; Defensive end, end
Military: US Army
Packers: 1941, 44-45
After football: Warehouse supervisor for Buckeye Furniture in Toledo, Ohio
Died: September 7, 2007
City: Toledo, Ohio

Ray Wehba

Born: August 16, 1916
City: Sherman, Texas
College: USC
Size: 6-0, 215; End
Packers: 1944; also played with the Brooklyn Dodgers in 1943
Died: June 2, 2003
City: Downey, California

Acknowledgements

The editing, design and publishing of this book is the work of Mike Dauplaise, M&B Global Solutions Inc. of Green Bay.

Appreciation is also directed to the *Green Bay Press-Gazette* photographers who captured the scenes that helped bring the story of Green Bay and the Packers of 1944 to life. Photos were also supplied by the University of Wisconsin-Green Bay Research Center, the Green Bay Packers, and the University of Wisconsin-Platteville.

About the Author

Tony Walter is a retired reporter, columnist and editor for the *Green Bay Press-Gazette* and was on the prototype team for *USA Today* in 1981. His journalism journey includes an on-field assignment during the 1967 NFL Championship Game, known as the Ice Bowl, and a one-on-one interview with Barack Obama. This is his fourth book pertaining to Green Bay Packers history.

www.ingramcontent.com/pod-product-compliance
Lightning Source LLC
Chambersburg PA
CBHW070056080526
44586CB00013B/1079